Robert Cartwright

The Footsteps of Shakspere

Or, a ramble with the early dramatists, containing much new and interesting

information respecting Shakspere, Lyly, Marlowe, Greene, and others

Robert Cartwright

The Footsteps of Shakspere
Or, a ramble with the early dramatists, containing much new and interesting information respecting Shakspere, Lyly, Marlowe, Greene, and others

ISBN/EAN: 9783337303198

Printed in Europe, USA, Canada, Australia, Japan

Cover: Foto ©Thomas Meinert / pixelio.de

More available books at **www.hansebooks.com**

CONTAI

INTER

SPEC

LY, M

AND OTHE

LONDON:
RUSSELL SMITH,
36, SOHO SQUARE.
M.DCCC.LXII.

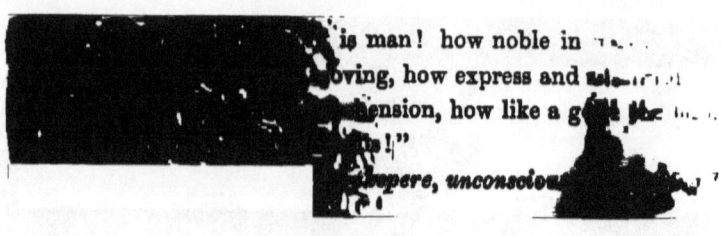

"In Hamlet he seems to have wished to exemplify the moral necessity of a due balance between our attention to the objects of our senses, and our meditation on the workings of our minds, an equilibrium between the real and the imaginary worlds. In Hamlet this balance is disturbed; his thoughts and the images of his fancy are far more vivid than his actual perceptions, and his very perceptions, instantly passing through the *medium* of his contemplations, acquire, as they pass, a form and a colour, not naturally their own. Hence we see a great, an almost enormous intellectual activity, and a proportional aversion to real action, consequent upon it, with all its symptoms and accompanying qualities. This character Shakspere places in circumstances under which it is obliged to act on the spur of the moment:—Hamlet is brave and careless of death; but he vacillates from sensibility, and procrastinates from thought, and loses the power of action in the energy of resolve."

Coleridge, unconsciously describing h

TO

E GHOST OF APOLLO,

OSE SONS, POETICAL OR MEDICAL,

ARE MOST CANTANKEROUS FELLOWS,

A MOST SWEET DISCORD.

---

being acquainted with any parties critically
sant with Elizabethan literature, I am urged by a
f duty, like Nelson, or rather with the devotion
Curtius, to publish these discoveries, be they true
iginary; I have no theories to defend, and can
subscribe to the words of the Reverend Mr.

"I have anywhere used the unbecoming language
olute certainty, or assumed the unauthorized tone
tation to others,—I would plead, in bar of judg-
the difficulty of conveying the result of one's own
ction, [and without conviction, such an essay were
pertinence not to be excused] without either
ing over-confident, or employing *such a multi-
y of words and forms of deprecation* as would
mount to a worse abuse of the Liberty of
Pre-ANT That I think I have arrived at a true
ion appearance in print is sufficient evidence."

ber *ision; Shakspere Society.*

I would also gladly join the reverend gentleman in the following request, "I shall be deeply obliged to any one who will *kindly* set me right;" but, oh ye gods, fond idea, how precious green!—nothing can slake the rabid thirst for revenge, nothing can mollify the wounded prejudices of a Shaksperian critic;—oh prophetic soul! I see myself rushing, like Cain, into the house of destruction, into a den of murder, like France's England, a hotbed of assassins;—

> Woe's me, woe's me; Apollo, oh, Apollo!
> Save me from their knives and tomahawks;
> Save me from these critical savages.
> Oh, Apollo!
> God " of physicke and of poesie,"
> Give *me*—thy blessing.

that hath saved thy life, says Marlowe;* and so say all my critics, kindness and forgiveness beaming in their celestial visages; or as a pilgrim at a higher shrine than Apollo's hath sung:—

> "But mercy is above this scepter'd sway,
> It is enthroned in the hearts of kings,
> It is an attribute to God himself;
> And *critic's* power doth then show likest God's
> When mercy seasons justice."

---

* *Vide Annotation*, page 27.

CONTENTS.

Was Shakspere a Lawyer's Clerk?	1
Shakspere's Latin	9
What was Shakspere's Occupation before going to London?	13
Annotations	14
Hamlet	34
Shakspere's Greek	77
Hamlet, Biron, &c.	87
Lyly's Endymion	91
All's Well that Ends Well	99
Lyly's Sapho and Phao, Campaspe, Gallathea	101
Love's Labour's Lost	103
Lyly's Midas	105
Pericles	115
Spenser, Henry VI., Romeo and Juliet	118
Merry Wives of Windsor	124
Thomas Nash	133
Christopher Marlowe	138
Robert Greene	146
The Sonnets	154
Midsummer Night's Dream	159
Edward III.	175
Merchant of Venice, Taming of the Shrew, Taming of a Shrew, King John, Henry V.	179

THE
FOOTSTEPS OF SHAKSPERE.

On reading in January, 1859, a paragraph in a newspaper, that Lord Campbell was about publishing some remarks on Shakspere's Legal Acquirements, it struck me, as an interesting occupation for a leisure hour, to examine into the subject beforehand, and see how far my own opinions might coincide with those of the Judge. As it is believed by some, though disbelieved by others, that Shakspere, before going to London, was for several years a lawyer's clerk at Stratford, it may be presumed, if such were the case, his legal phraseology and imagery would be most abundant in his earlier plays; and I cannot give the result of my investigation more concisely and distinctly, than by commenting on a few extracts from his Lordship's book.

"The great difficulty is to discover, or to conjecture, with reasonable probability, how Shakspere was employed from about 1579, when he most likely left school, until about 1586, when he is supposed to have gone to London."

Shakspere's actual occupations during these important years, when his character was formed, there is not a *scintilla* of contemporary proof."

"An attorney's clerk,"—"first suggested by Chalmers and since countenanced by Malone, yourself, &c.," "but impugned by nearly an equal number of biographers and critics of almost equal authority."

"We should only have to recollect the maxim, that the vessel long retains the flavour with which it has been once imbued."

"In *Two Gentlemen of Verona, Pericles of Tyre,* and *Titus Andronicus,* &c. in fourteen of the thirty-seven dramas generally attributed to Shakspere,—I find nothing that fairly bears upon this controversy."

It may here be remarked, that *no "flavour" in the first three plays* ought to be considered, according to Lord Campbell's own showing, strong presumptive evidence, Shakspere could not have been a lawyer's clerk at Stratford.

But let us see what law phrases and allusions are to be found in these plays :—

Thaliard. "For if a king bid a man be a villain, he is bound by the indenture of his oath to be one."—
Pericles, act i., scene 3.

2nd. Fish. "Help, master, help; here's a fish hangs in the net, like a poor man's right in the law; 'twill hardly come out."—*Pericles,* act ii., scene 1.

Prot. "That they are out by lease."—
Two Gentlemen of Verona, act v., scene 2.

Tit. "I did my lord, yet let me be their bail to answer their suspicion."—*Titus Andronicus,* act ii., scene 4.

If there be any more law-phrases in these three plays, they are so few and trivial as to have escaped observation.

We will now proceed to another extract from his Lordship's book :—

> "*Hamlet.* In this tragedy various expressions and allusions crop out, showing the substratum of law in the author's mind,"
> "Nor will it yield to Norway or the Pole
> A ranker rate, *should it be sold in fee.*"

and,

> "Why such impress of shipwrights, whose sore task
> Does not divide the Sunday from the week."

"this passage has been quoted by Judges on the bench as an authority upon the press-gang, and upon the debated question whether shipwrights as well as *common sea-men* are liable to be pressed into the service of the royal navy."

"The discussion as to whether Ophelia was entitled to Christian burial, proves that Shakspere had read and studied Plowden's Report of the celebrated case of Hales *v.* Petit, tried in the reign of Philip and Mary, and that he intended to ridicule the counsel who argued, and the Judges who decided it. Upon an inquisition before the Coroner, a verdict of *felo de se* was returned. Under this finding, his body was to be buried in a cross-road, with a stake thrust through it, and all his goods were forfeited to the crown."

"Hamlet's own speech, &c., abounds with lawyer-like thoughts and words."

The having "studied Plowden's Report and the ridiculing of the counsel and of the Judges" no more proves Shakspere to have been a lawyer's clerk, than that a novelist, who ridicules the contradictory evidence of medical men in a case of poisoning, must necessarily have been an apothecary's apprentice. I shall here give Hamlet's speech according to the first edition, 1603, as being more suitable to the present inquiry:—

Ham. Look you, there's another Horatio,
Why mai't not be the skull of some lawyer?
Methinks he should indite that fellow
Of an action of Batterie, for knocking
Him about the pate with's shovel, now where is your
Quirkes and quillets now, your vouchers and
Double vouchers, your leases and free-holde,
And tenements? why that same boxe there will scarce
Holde the conveiance of his land, and must
The honor lie there? O pittiful transformance!
I prethee tell me Horatio,
Is parchment made of sheep-skinnes?
Hor. I my Lorde, and of calves-skinnes too.
Ham. I faith they prove themselves sheepe and calves
That deale with them, or put their trust in them."

It may here be objected, this speech proves too much for the advocates of the attorney's office; the writer must have been a practised lawyer, or else, student-like, he picked the various terms and phrases out of a book, and so concocted the speech. As there is scarcely an atom of law in the three preceding plays, it is contrary to all probability Shakspere should have "*bottled up*" *his law for three whole years,* and then suddenly burst out, like Minerva from Jupiter's head, a full-blown lawyer.

Let us examine the chronology of the first six plays; *Pericles, Two Gentlemen of Verona,* and *Titus Andronicus,* are acknowledged to be the first three. Hamlet was certainly in existence in 1589, and most probably written in '88; in act fifth, scene first, Hamlet says, "By the Lord, Horatio, these three years I have taken note of it; the age is grown so picked, that the toe of the peasant comes so near the heel of the courtier, he galls his kibe;" and again, " For O, for O, the hobby horse is forgot." Now in *Love's Labour's Lost* is the following passage:—

Arm. How hast thou purchased this experience?
Moth. By my penny of observation.
Arm. But O,—but O.—
Moth. — the hobby horse is forgot.
Act iii., scene 1.

It is therefore evident, these two plays were intimately connected together in the poet's mind, and must have been produced about the same time. That the comedy followed the tragedy, may be inferred from its containing an allusion to Bank's dancing horse, exhibited in London in 1589.

As the *Comedy of Errors* contains an allusion to the civil contests in France, which followed upon the assassination of Henry III, in August, 1589, it was most probably written after *Love's Labour's Lost*. In this latter play we find there is a sprinkling of law, but in the *Comedy of Errors* the poet luxuriates, riots in legal jokes and quibbles, like a whale off Wick gambolling amongst the herrings, " very like a whale."

As all the other plays, the *Poems* as well as the *Sonnets*,* were written at a later period, it is unnecessary to refer to them. We may therefore sum up:—there is not in the first three plays a *scintilla* of evidence, that Shakspere had been a lawyer's clerk; in the fourth and

---

* I have proved *clearly and concisely*, that the *Sonnets* extend over the period from 1591 to 1596, *vide The Sonnets of Shakspere, rearranged*. London, J. Russell Smith, 1859.

fifth, *Hamlet* and *Love's Labour's Lost*, there is sufficient to justify the supposition; but in the last, the *Comedy of Errors*, he rejoices in "the professional jokes of the attorney's office in great abundance." Such circumstantial evidence forces upon us the conviction, Shakspere commenced the study of the law after he went to London, and probably only a few months previous to the composition of *Hamlet;* and it may be added, not only Hamlet's speech, but all the knowledge he displayed of the law in these three plays, leads to the inference that he first took to the study thereof, not merely from his love of universal knowledge, but also "professionally," as it furnished not only instructive matter, but food in abundance for jokes and quibbles to please the million.

Having now made a searching examination into the first six plays, we are better enabled to judge what value should be set on a certain celebrated Epistle; *vide* Lord Campbell's book, p. 26:—

"An Epistle to the Gentlemen Students of the Two Universities, by Thomas Nash," prefixed to the first edition of Robert Greene's Menaphon, in 1589. The alleged libel on Shakspere is in the words following:—

" I will turn back to my first text of studies of delight, and talk a little in friendship with a few of our trivial translators. It is a common practice now-a-days, amongst a sort of shifting companions that run thro' every art, and thrive by none, to leave the trade of Noverint, whereto they were born, and busy themselves with the endeavours of art, that could scarcely Latinize their neck-verse if they should have need; yet English Seneca, read by candle light, yields many good sentences, as *blood is a beggar*, and so forth; and if you intreat him fair, in a frosty morning, he will afford you whole Hamlets; I should say handfuls of tragical speeches. But O grief! *Tempus edax rerum*—what is that will always last? The sea exhaled by drops will in continuance be dry; and Seneca, let blood, line by line, and page by page, at length must needs die to our stage."

Presuming that this epistle is a personal attack on Shakspere, we know, the great "endeavour of art" in such writings is so to word the article, that it shall read at the first glance complimentary, and yet be full of spiteful and offensive allusions; the writer also shows still greater skill, if he can season it with a few lies, having an air of truth. This epistle is a masterpiece of the kind; for one set of critics contend it does not refer to Shakspere personally; that Nash alludes only to playwrights, who busy themselves with the endeavour of art in adopting sentences from Seneca so as to *rival whole Hamlets* in tragical speeches;—evidently complimentary. But others consider Shakspere is the party alluded to, and hence arose the supposition he had been a lawyer's clerk.

Nash may have been misled by Hamlet's apparently intimate knowledge of the law; and yet as the public might naturally suppose the author had been brought up to the law, the assertion may have been an intentional falsehood; but it was a master-stroke to insinuate the tragical speeches were purloined from an English Seneca; and the sneer about not being able to " Latinize his neck-verse if it should be needful" must have had a telling effect upon the Gentlemen Students of the two Universities.

As this epistle is thus evidently written with the most cunning malevolence, we are no more justified in believing, on its authority, Shakspere had been a lawyer's clerk, than that the tragical speeches are purloined from Seneca, and that he could not, at this time, 1589, Latinize his neck-verse. It is gratifying to find these views corroborated by the concluding remarks of the learned Judge;—" But, my dear Mr. Payne Collier,—still I must warn you, that I myself remain rather sceptical; their statement that he had belonged to the profession of the law may be as false as that he was a plagiarist from Seneca. Nash and Robert Greene may have invented it or repeated it on some groundless rumour."

I have no doubt that Nash is Guildenstern or Rosencrantz, and Greene the other; for we cannot suppose the latter would have allowed Nash to prefix such an epistle to *Menaphon,* unless he also had had a quarrel with Shakspere. This epistle is the retort courteous to our gentle Willy; it is highly interesting to see the infant Hercules in the very struggles of his contest with the two serpents, " whom I will trust, as I will adders fanged;" the one on this occasion, hissed, gnashed, and showed his fangs; the other in 1592, spat his venom out and died;—it is worthy of note, that in neither instance is there a word against Shakspere's private character.

There is every reason to believe, that Shakspere, on going to London, was extremely deficient in a knowledge of Latin. Jonson says, "he had small Latin and less Greek"; and it is very remarkable, in the first two plays the classical allusions are few and trivial, the ordinary stock of a school boy; in *Pericles*, Jove, Juno, Diana, Cynthia, Neptune; Lucina and Æsculapius have the flavour of the doctor's shop; in the *Two Gentlemen of Verona*, the Hellespont, Elysium, Hero's tower and bold Leander, Phaëton, and Orpheus;

"Madam, 'twas Ariadne passioning
For Theseus' perjury, and unjust flight,"

perhaps denotes, he had already commenced his studies. But *Titus Andronicus* is a Roman play, and in all probability selected for the special purpose of showing off his classical acquirements; and it should be noticed, this classical ornamentation is taken entirely from the *Ænied* and *Ovid's Metamorphoses*. There is also such a marked distinction in this play from the others in style, that Hallam says, "it is not Shakspere's in any sense"; but that does not at all follow; there is a similar difference between the Venus and Adonis and the Lucrece, altho' only one year elapsed between them. It may be reasonably conjectured, that *Titus Andronicus* is a more laboured production; that our poet having produced the best comedy, made an ambitious effort to surpass his rivals in the higher and sublimer regions of tragedy; that a young and comparatively uneducated poet should in his twenty-third year mistake the blood and murder, the horrors of the barbarian school for the true sublime, is not to be wondered at; especially when we reflect, that for two centuries the master-pieces of the human intellect have been regarded, not only by foreigners but by his own countrymen, as the productions of a wild and irregular genius, deficient in judgment and taste. But now it is advanced, that Plato and Socrates had prefigured in their minds the plays of Shakspere as the highest form of the drama, and truest to nature :—

"It is truly singular," says Coleridge, "that Plato, genuine prophet and anticipator as he was of the Protestant Christian Era, should have given in his *Dialogue of the Banquet*, a justification of our Shakspere; for he relates that, when all the other guests had either dispersed or fallen asleep, Socrates only, together with Aristophanes and Agathon, remained awake; and that, while he continued to drink with them out of a large goblet, he compelled them, tho' most reluctantly, to admit that it was the business of one and the same genius to excel in tragic and comic poetry, or that the tragic poet ought, at the same time, to contain within himself the powers of comedy," *Remains,* vol. xi., p. 12; and further on he writes, p. 63, "I own I am proud that I was the first in time who publicly demonstrated to the full extent of the position, that the supposed irregularity and extravagancies of Shakspere were the mere dreams of a pedantry that arraigned the eagle because it had not the dimensions of the swan;—the judgment of Shakspere is commensurate with his genius."

It may then be taken for granted, that Skakspere on going to London and being thrown into the society of University men, felt conscious, perhaps galled and ashamed, of his deficiencies in classical literature; that he spent some time in a diligent application to those studies, and acquired the power of reading the Latin authors with facility. Latin composition, verses, and discourses, he probably regarded as sheer pedantry, dilettantism, a lamentable waste of useful time; as Biron says:—

> " Small have continual plodders ever won,
> Save base authority from others' books;"

in *Hamlet* he says, Seneca is heavy and Plautus light, and gives in the character of Laertes a sly rap at the University man, who could only express his grief for his sister's loss by calling on Pelion and Olympus to fall upon him; his classical knowledge, or at least the display thereof, culminates in *Love's Labour's Lost*; although it again bursts forth in the first part of *Henry VI*, probably in consequence of Nash's spiteful epistle.

It has been said, that in the *Two Gentlemen of Verona* we see "the germ of other plays, or rather, the germ of some other of his most admired characters," so it may be said, that in *Titus Andronicus* we see the classical allusions of future works;—apart from the beautiful passages quoted by Mr. Knight in his valuable *Notice on the Authenticity of Titus Andronicus*, the following extracts may be adduced as not only additional evidence that Shakspere was the author, but that he also wrote the play, *Dido and Æneas*, referred to in Hamlet:—

> " To bid Æneas tell the tale twice o'er,
> How Troy was burnt, and he made miserable?"

"And I have read that Hecuba of Troy
   Ran mad through sorrow."

"So pale did shine the moon on Pyramus,
   When he by night lay bath'd in maiden blood."

"As Cerberus at the Thracian poet's feet."

          "As Tarquin erst
That left the camp to sin in Lucrece bed."
"Take this of me, Lucrece was not more chaste
Than this Lavinia, Bassianus' love."

The following lines are also Shaksperian :—

"Romans, friends, followers, favourers of my right."
"Gracious Lavinia, Rome's rich ornament."

"Wilt thou draw near the nature of the gods?
   Draw near them then in being merciful:
   Sweet mercy is nobility's true badge."

"What, hast not thou full often struck a doe,
   And borne her cleanly by the keeper's nose."

"She is a woman, therefore may be woo'd;
   She is a woman, therefore may be won;
   She is Lavinia, therefore must be lov'd."

"Oh! had the monster seen those lily hands
   Tremble like aspen leaves upon a lute,
   And make the silken strings delight to kiss them."

The last two extracts may be compared with the following :—

"How oft, when thou, my music, music play'st, &c.,
   Do I envy those jacks, that nimble leap
      To kiss the tender inward of thy hand."
Sonnet 130.

Suf. "She's beautiful; and therefore to be woo'd;
   She is a woman; therefore to be won."—
Henry VI., act v., scene 3.

Glo. "Was ever woman in this humour woo'd?
   Was ever woman in this humour won?"—
Richard III.

What was Shakspere's occupation before going to London?

"Of Shakspere's actual occupations during these important years, when *his character was formed*, there is not a *scintilla* of contemporary proof." "Nay, notwithstanding the admonition to be found in his works, 'Throw physic to the dogs,' it has been *gravely* suggested, that he must have been initiated in medicine, from the minute inventory of the contents of the apothecary's shop in *Romeo and Juliet.*"—*Shakspere's Legal Acquirements.*

The gravity of the Bench relaxes into a smile, but it is not safe for a man living in a glass house to throw stones;—what says young Hamlet?—

"I' faith they prove themselves sheepe and calves
   That deale with them, or put their trust in them."

When I first entered upon the inquiry, "Had Shakspere

been a lawyer's clerk?" I commenced with *Romeo and Juliet* under the impression it was one of his earlier plays; and I cannot express my surprise, as the further I proceeded, the more strong became my conviction, he must, at some period or other, have studied medicine; for the whole play breathes of it—is instinct with the spirit thereof. But as it was written in 1591, it can be of no value as evidence, whether he studied medicine before or after settling in London. Let us, then, examine the first six plays with reference to this point, but in the reverse order, beginning with the last, and ending with "Shakspere's own muse his Pericles first bore."

In the *Comedy of Errors* there is but little physic, just sufficient to show the author was conversant with the subject. In *Love's Labour's Lost,* physic predominates over law. Armado's letter to the king is adduced by Lord Campbell as being "drawn up in the true lawyer-like tautological dialect;—no ordinary man could have hit it off so exactly without having *engrossed* in an attorney's office;" but the commencement of the letter hits off the medical language of the period just as accurately; "So it is beseiged with sable-coloured melancholy, I did commend the black oppressing humour to the most wholesome physic of the health-giving air, and, as I am a gentleman, betook myself to walk." The first scene in the second act is full of medical jokes:—

    Moth. "A wonder, master; here's a Costard broken in the shin.
    Cost. No salve, sir, but a plantain.
    Arm. We will talk no more of this matter.
    Moth. Till there be more matter in the shin.
    Arm. Thou wer't immured, restrained, captivated, bound.

Cost. True, true; and now you will give me my purgation, and let me loose."

In act fourth, scene second, we read:—*Hol.* "This is a gift that I have; simple, simple, a foolish extravagant spirit, full of forms, figures, shapes, objects, ideas, apprehensions, motives, revolutions; these are begot in the ventricle of memory, nourished in the womb of *pia mater,* and deliver'd upon the mellowing of occasion." It may be said, "no ordinary man could have hit it off so exactly without having" *dissected* in a school of medicine. Rosaline's advice to Biron is a medical lecture, and he replies, "I'll jest a twelvemonth in an hospital." It is very evident, that in this play, physic predominates over law. It should also be here mentioned, that the language of Armado is not very different from that of Andrew Borde, the physician, who, according to Hearne, gave rise to the name of Merry Andrew, the fool of the mountebank stage. His *Breviary of Health,* first printed in 1547, begins thus: " Egregious doctours and maysters of the eximious and archane science of physicke, of your urbanitie exasperate not your selve."—*Pictorial Shakspere.*

Hamlet is, like *Romeo and Juliet,* undeniably a medical production, and could only have been written by one who had studied the philosophy of medicine, particularly psychology; and whilst "the various expressions and allusions, which crop out, show the substratum of *physic* in the author's mind," and give to the play life and nature, the legal allusions and expressions are merely so many weeds, and the whole crop might be weeded out without injury, if not with benefit.

Ophelia's song is further evidence of Shakspere's professional studies, as it is not uncommon in virtuous young women for insanity to take an erotic form. "The pregnant hinges of the knee" has been quoted by an eminent anatomist as proof, Shakspere must have *dissected;* and Hamlet's challenge :—

> "Woul't drink up Esil? eat a crocodile?
> I'll do't."

has a strong flavour of the doctor's shop, the one being a nauseously bitter draught, and the other, most likely, an equally filthy electuary.*

In *Titus Andronicus* it may be said, both law and physic are at a discount.

In the *Two Gentlemen of Verona* "various expressions and allusions crop out, showing the substratum of physic in the author's mind." Who but a medical student could have put into Julia's pretty lips :—

> "And here is writ—love-wounded Proteus ;—
> Poor wounded name! my bosom, as a bed,
> Shall lodge thee, till thy wound be thoroughly heal'd;
> And thus I *search* it with a *sovereign* kiss."

and Speed's jocularity is worthy of Guy's Hospital or the Edinburgh Infirmary :—

> *Speed.* "Without you? nay, that's certain, for without you were so simple, none else would; but you are so without

---

* Had Hamlet said, "Woul't drink up Esil? eat a *Pharaoh*," there never would have been a doubt on the subject, since the mummy was certainly used medicinally :—
  Gasp. "Your followers
       Have swallow'd you like mummia, and, being sick
       With such unnatural and horrid physic,
       Vomit you up i' the kennel."—Webster's *White Devil.*

these follies, that these follies are within you and shine through you like the water in an urinal; that not an eye that sees you but is a physician to comment on your malady."

Pericles:—the whole play is redolent of physic, of the apothecary's shop; not only Cerimon, but Pericles, Helicanus, Dionizza, and Marina, talk physic. As the three last acts are entirely medical, I must refer the reader to the play itself; the following extracts can answer for themselves:—

Cer. " I held it ever,
　　Virtue and cunning were endowments greater
　　Than nobleness and riches: careless heirs
　　May the two latter darken and expend;
　　But immortality attends the former,
　　Making a man a god. 'Tis known, I ever
　　Have studied physic, through which secret art,
　　By turning o'er authorities, I have
　　[Together with my practice] made familiar
　　To me and to my aid, the blest infusions
　　That dwell in vegatives, in metals, stones:
　　And I can speak of the disturbances
　　That nature works, and of her cures; which gives me
　　A more content in course of true delight
　　Than to be thirsty after tottering honour,
　　Or tie my treasure up in silken bags,
　　To please the Fool and Death."—
　　　　　　　　　　　　　Act iii., scene 2.

"Trivial as the sketch may be called of this good physician, it is a portrait; we see him, and we know him, though observed only under one phase. Here, in the recovery of the Queen from her trance, we have a most natural description of the physician's skill being suddenly called into action; his swift orders mingled with his reasoning on cases, his haste to apply the remedies, the broken sentences, his reproof to a loitering servant, the keeping the gentlemen back to 'give her air;' the whole, as if by magic, making the reader an absolute spectator of the scene."

"Compared to all that precedes it, or to anything else, the first scene of the fifth act is wonderfully grand, beautiful, and refined in art. Every one ought to know it; but it is too long for me to quote. The recall from a state of stupefaction caused by grief, and the prolonged, yet natural recognition of Marina, interwoven with a thousand delicate hues of poetry, lead us on in admiration, till we think nothing can be added to the effect. Still the crown of all is to come, in the poetical conclusion, true to nature while it rests on our imagination. Pericles, instantly after his sudden rush of joy, his overwrought excitement, fancies he listens to the 'music of the spheres!'—he wonders that others do not hear these 'rarest sounds;'—then he sinks on his couch to rest, and still insisting that there is 'most heavenly music,' falls into a sleep, while Marina, like an angel, watches at his side!"—*Ch. Armitage Brown*, p. 242.

To the great knowledge of medicine displayed in this production, as further proof of his early studies, may be added the following passage:—"He is bound by the indenture of his oath;" evidently the apprentice rejoices in the pleasure of soon being out of his indentures.

We may then sum up;—the first play is essentially medical, and could only have been written by one who had studied medicine; take away the scenes connected with Cerimon, Marina, and the stupor of Pericles, and the play dwindles to an idle story, a copy of juvenile verses in imitation of old Gower. In the second and fifth, the *Two Gentlemen of Verona* and *Love's Labour's Lost*, physic predominates over law;—whilst *Hamlet* could only have been written by one who had studied the philosophy of medicine. Thus, in four out of the first five plays, the doctor stands prominently forward; but the whole force and strength of the argument lies in the first two plays; there can be but one verdict,—*Pericles*, the play I was so fond of as a boy, settles the question, —Shakspere must have been "*during those important years, when his character was formed,*" an Apothecary's Apprentice; nor am I acquainted with any position in life more suitable for, and so completely in harmony with, the actual growth and development of his peculiarly practical and universal mind.

This conviction is powerfully corroborated by the following extract from Coleridge:—"For a young author's first work almost always bespeaks his recent pursuits; and his first observations of life are either drawn from the immediate employments of his youth, and from the characters and images most deeply impressed on his mind in the situation in which those employments had placed him; or else they are fixed on such objects and occurrences in the world as are easily connected with, and seem to bear upon, his studies and the hitherto exclusive subjects of his meditation. Just as Ben Jonson, who applied himself to the drama after having served in Flanders, fills his earliest plays with true or pretended soldiers, the wrongs and neglects of the former, and the absurd boasts and knavery of their counterfeits. So Lessing's first comedies are placed in the

Universities, and consist of events and characters conceivable in an academic life."—*Literary Remains*, vol. ii.

It should here be mentioned, that *All's Well that Ends Well* was written in the spring of 1587, and was corrected and augmented probably about 1599. In one of the most highly finished scenes we find the following legal phraseology:—

> *Par.* "Sir, for a *quart d'ecu* he will sell the fee-simple of his salvation, the inheritance of it; and cut the entail from all remainders, and a perpetual succession for it perpetually."—
> Act iv., scene 3.

Even if this passage had been in the original sketch, it would have been no evidence of Shakspere having been a lawyer's clerk; since it is preceded by three plays, in which there are only trifling allusions to the law; but as the comedy is founded upon the story of a young lady, the daughter of a physician, curing the King of France with a celebrated prescription of her father's, it does serve as corroborative evidence to the two preceding plays, abounding in medical allusions.

Thus, after a close and searching examination of these plays, we light on the interesting fact, that Shakspere in his youth had been, not a lawyer's clerk, but an apothecary's apprentice. How mysterious are the ways of Providence; how far beyond the ken of common minds! What possible situation in life could Fortune's dearest spite have dropped him into, so suitable for the growth and development of his bodily and mental powers? Active exercise and mental culture; a neophyte in the temple of nature, soon to be her great High Priest! At first, as a lesson in humility, he sweeps the shop and dusts the bottles; then gains a practical knowledge of chemical compounds, and studies botany, not lazily in a botanic garden, but practically, rambling through the fields and woods, collecting medicinal plants, thus sucking the milk of knowledge direct from the breasts of nature. Then doctoring the stable-boys at the Hall or Castle, he becomes knowing in horse-flesh, hounds, and hawks; tea's with the house-keeper, wine's with the butler, so learns heraldry and chaffing with the maids;—then called up at night to a labour, he hurries to the patient in town or country; the baby's squalls appeased, and the mother comfortable, pleased and thankful that all is well, he homewards takes his way, musing now on earthly, now on heavenly things; now gazing at the glorious morning star, an orb ne'er seen nor dreamt of by the lawyer's clerk; if seen, mistaken for the moon; if dreamt of, 'tis the chancellor's wig.

As the proper study of mankind is man, and Shakspere *did* man as effectually as any tourist does the Rhine or Switzerland; what could he learn of man in a lawyer's office, save the meanness and selfishness of his character; whilst in the same worldly-minded creature, stretched on the bed of sickness, oft the nobler feelings of our nature are displayed, as well as in the kindly offices of that ministering angel, woman; thus, like a beautiful rose-bud, daily absorbing fresh juices and odours, healthily grew and expanded Shakspere's mind in the doctor's shop.

At what time he quitted medicine for the stage is uncertain; but he certainly did not do so, as ill-natured people said, from a love of idleness and pleasure, but in obedience to an internal impulse—an urgent, imperative law of nature; not but that he also acted with perfect freewill; for being well aware, that success in the medical trade does not depend on professional skill and abilities, nor on kindness and attention, but on other arts unnecessary here to mention, he wisely cut the doctor's shop and took to the theatre, just as a duckling, though nursed by a hen, instinctively takes to the water; and thus, fate and freewill acting harmoniously together, England for once had the right man in the right place.

Thus the two great difficulties; his hurried marriage, and his going to London without his wife, are satisfactorily cleared up by the fact of his having been an apothecary's apprentice. The hurried marriage (about which, says the Rev. G. Gilfillan, a deal of nonsense has been uttered, arising from a confusion of marriage with the then common practice of previous betrothal), may be easily explained on the supposition, Shakspere got leave of absence for a few days, as his master could not dispense with his services for a longer period. It may also be reasonably conjectured, that Shakspere, as soon as he was out of his indentures in April, 1585, instead of going to London to walk the hospitals and study for the Hall, went immediately under an engagement to the Blackfriars Theatre, being related to one of the performers, Thomas Greene, his fellow-townsman. Mrs. William certainly could not have accompanied him on this first trip, as she had been confined of twins only a few weeks previously.

Our poet has with a grateful feeling, that does him

honour, portrayed his good and learned master under the character of Cerimon in *Pericles,* and again as Friar Lawrence in *Romeo and Juliet;* but the half-starved Apothecary at Mantua is, I am sorry to say, doctorlike, a malicious description of the opposition-shop at Stratford. This account is confirmed by the following extract from Mr. Knight's *Biography,* p. 183, in which he gives, though unintentionally, a most accurate description of that nearly extinct animal, the ancient apothecary:—"The kind old man, going forth from his cell in the evening twilight to fill his osier basket with weeds and flowers, and moralising on the properties of plants, which at once yield poison and medicine, has all the truth of individual portraiture; and the young Shakspere *may have known* some kindly old man, full of axiomatic wisdom, and sufficiently confident in his own management, like the well-meaning Friar Lawrence."

Joseph Warton also makes a very striking observation on the passage, "I do remember an apothecary," which is well parried by Mr. Knight in his illustration, but, as usual, the truth lies *in medio*. Warton objects that Romeo, to remember these terms, must *think;* but the fact is, the items came naturally, uncalled for, into his mind; for was he not an apothecary's apprentice? thus the speech is highly appropriate and characteristic; but the critics, not being aware of this fact, are quite at sea on this occasion as on several others. "I appeal to those," says Warton, "who know anything of the human heart, whether Romeo, in this distressed situation, could have leisure to think of the alligator, empty boxes and bladders, and other furniture of this beggarly shop, and to point them out so distinctly to the audience. The description is, indeed, very lively and natural, but very improperly put into the mouth of a person agitated with such passion as Romeo is represented to be." "What, then," replies Mr. Knight, "had he leisure to do? Had he leisure to run off into declamations against fate, &c. From the moment he had said, 'Well, Juliet, I will lie with you to-night. Let's see for means,' the apothecary's shop became to him the object of the most intense interest."—Delightful treat to see a well-fought battle between romanticist and classicist!

The tradition of the Royal College of Surgeons, that Shakspere had been a barber-surgeon, and stuck up his pole next door to the Boar's Head, Eastcheap, is scarcely tenable; nor can it be traced to an earlier period than about the middle of the last century. Nor can Shakspere's fondness for amputations, or rather decapitations, verbal as well as corporal, be adduced as evidence of his surgical skill; other playwrights did the same, and even more freely; they merely followed the example of her Majesty's gracious government in those happy days. Nor could he have been the pupil of a physician, nor of an incumbent licensed by the bishop to practise medicine, since in either case he would certainly have been advised and encouraged to become a proficient in classical literature. The question is thus reduced to its narrowest compass; Shakspere must have been *"during those important years when his character was formed,"*

AN APOTHECARY'S APPRENTICE,
THE STUDENT OF NATURE.

I take this opportunity of proposing the following explanation of a passage in the *Two Gentlemen of Verona*, which has much perplexed the commentators:—

> *Val.* "And that my love may appear plain and free,
>   All that was mine in Silvia, I give thee.
> *Jul.* O me, unhappy!   [*Faints.*
> *Pro.* Look to the boy."—
>   Act v., scene 4.

"I give thee" means I *forgive* thee, and should have been printed "I 'give thee;" Valentine says to his penitent friend, I forgive you not only my banishment, &c., but since

> "Who by repentance is not satisfied,
>   Is nor of heaven nor earth,"

therefore, to prove the sincerity of my love and forgiveness in the strongest form possible, I forgive all you have done against Silvia, a far more unpardonable offence than any personal injury to myself. Valentine, who had just overheard Silvia's declaration of her passionate love for himself, and her detestation of his friend, could never have dreamt of giving his sweetheart to Proteus, nor was she one to submit to be given away so easily, she hath-a-way of her own; and shortly afterwards Valentine says:—

> "Thurio, give back, or else embrace thy death;
>   Come not within the measure of my wrath;
>   Do not name Silvia thine; if once again,
>   Milan shall not behold thee."

No sooner has Valentine forgiven his friend, than Julia, exclaiming, "O me, unhappy!" *pretends* to faint; and then, by giving to Proteus his own ring, the sly baggage brings about an *eclaircissement* at a most auspicious moment, when her lover was in a soft and repentant mood; for is not Julia, though a warm-hearted girl, a cunning gipsy too? Does she not tell fibs in saying, she "neglected to deliver a ring to madam Silvia?"—

Jul. "Madam, he sends your ladyship this ring."—
Act iv., scene 4.

Did she not, also, in the first act, favour us with an insight into her character by refusing the love-letter, and then playing tricks to get a peep at it?—

"How angrily I taught my brow to frown,
When inward joy enforc'd my heart to smile!"

This play, the *Two Gentlemen of Verona*, is of singular value in assisting us to gain a knowledge of Shakspere's heart as well as of his mind; not because it contains the "germ of other plays," but inasmuch as it contains a passage foreshadowing a page in the history of his own life; when, a few years after, his own friend and mistress happily behave false to him; he again, for is not Valentine, Shakspere, forgives his friend:—

"Ah! but those tears are pearl, which thy love sheds,
And they are rich, and ransom all ill deeds."

Valentine's expression, "I 'give thee," reminds us of a passage in the *Jew of Malta*, act i.:—

Abig. "Father, forgive me—"

in the *note* we read,

forgive me—] Old ed.: "give *me*—"

it does not follow, that *give* is here a misprint for *for-*

give; most probably Abigail, agonised at her father's violent language, was about exclaiming:—

"Give *me* thy blessing,"

as Barabas had just said:—

"I charge thee on my blessing that thou leave
These devils and their damned heresy!"

assuredly the old edition gives the correct reading; one touch of nature in Marlowe.

Ghost. "I find thee apt;
And duller should'st thou be than the fat weed
That roots itself in ease on Lethe wharf,
Would'st thou not stir in this."—
Hamlet, act i., scene 5.

"The fat weed" is undoubtedly the *henbane,* a narcotic; the whole plant is covered with unctuous fetid hairs. It is found in great abundance in Oxfordshire, and is here poetically and appropriately located on Lethe's bank. "The fat weed that roots itself in ease" is a most graphic description of the plant, and as it is the reading of the quartos, *rots* must consequently be regarded as a misprint in the folio.

Cymbeline. The speeches of the spirits and of Jupiter, in the vision of Posthumus, are not only universally acknowledged to be an interpolation of the players, but they are also directly opposed to the conception of the poet, who intended the dream to be a dumb show, like the vision of Katharine in *Henry VIII.* This is proved by the speech of Posthumus at the end, and by a speech at the opening of the play:—

> 1 *Gent.* " I cannot delve him to the root. His father
> Was called Sicilius, &c.;
> And had, besides this gentleman in question,
> Two other sons, who, in the wars o' the time,
> Died with their swords in hand."

Thus, the audience would readily recognise the spirits, and when Jupiter throws his thunderbolt, the book or label is supposed to fall on the bosom of Posthumus; Jupiter re-ascends, and the ghosts vanish. The vision consequently, is an integral part; but it is to be hoped future editors will expunge the fustian from this beautiful drama.

> *Fer.* " This is a most majestic vision, and
> Harmonious charmingly. May I be bold
> To think these spirits?
> *Pro.* Spirits, which by mine art
> I have from their confines called to enact
> My present fancies.
> *Fer.* Let me live here ever;
> So rare a wonder'd father, and a wife,
> Make this place paradise."—
> *Tempest,* act iv., scene 1.

Charmingly, or by *magic,* is contra-indicated by the subsequent question and answer; if Ferdinand knew it was all magic, the question and answer are unnecessary, mere tautology; *charming lays,* sanctioned by Gifford, Johnson, and others, is far preferable, and in all probability the true reading. Ferdinand is charmed not only by the splendour of the scene, but also by the song, and by the beautiful verses of Iris and Ceres, which were probably performed in recitative music.

The last passage is evidently corrupt; the masque has just been enacted, "a contract of true love to celebrate," and Ferdinand naturally and gallantly exclaims:—

"A wonder'd father, and so rare a wife,
Make this place paradise."

Wonder'd, wonderful, able to do wonders.

Ari. "Where the bee sucks, there suck I;
In a cowslip's bell I lie;
There I couch when owls do cry:
On the bat's back I do fly,
After sunset, merrily.
Merrily, merrily, shall I live now,
Under the blossom that hangs on the bow."—
Tempest, act v., scene 1.

Ariel, during the mid-day heat, or his custom of an afternoon, takes his siesta in a cowslip's bell; sleeps there at night; and, like other fashionables in Milan and Naples, promenades after sunset.

The usual reading, "*after summer,*" is a misprint, caused by the repetition of the word *merrily*. No naturalist could possibly have committed such a blunder as, "on a bat's back I do fly after summer," though he might have written on a *swift's* back; but then he could scarcely have added "merrily," for it would be no joke to sit a swallow :—

"The swallow follows not summer more willing, than we your lordship."—*Timon*, act iii., scene 6.

Ariel is nearly related to Puck; he evidently loves a bit of mischief, and enjoys the fun of leading Caliban and his companions into "the filthy mantled pool;" and his riding on a bat's back after sunset is a specimen of his humour, an image as full of playfulness as a kitten or a puppy-dog running after its tail.

"Flying after summer" may be a very fine idea, but it destroys the illusion of the scene, the domesticity of the isle; and is besides, inconsistent with the simplicity of Ariel's character, who is thinking only of his present happiness. In this pretty song about *cowslips and blossoms,* Ariel is describing the *merry* month of May, and perhaps the early part of June, in the neighbourhood of London or around Stratford; consequently, if he flies after anything, it must be after the spring, and not after the summer; in the middle of May, cowslip wine is made, and by the end of June how fares it with the blossom that hangs on the bough of the lime-tree?

As the *Tempest* was first printed in the folio of 1623, the error remained unnoticed till Theobald proposed *sunset,* and Mr. Hunter in his *Illustrations,* appears inclined to adopt it; even the prefix *Cer.* to the Song in the Masque was wanting, till Theobald made that important correction.

On looking over some of Mr. Staunton's annotations, I find he has anticipated me in the words *cumber'd* for *number'd* in *Cymbeline,* and *sheaf* for *cheff* or *chiefe* in *Hamlet* :—

"Of a most select and generous sheaf in that."

I had previously marked the passage in *Every Man out of his Humour,* but his extract from the *Magnetic Lady* is conclusive :—

"That it is found in noblemen and gentlemen
Of the best sheaf."—

Act iii., scene 4.

Perhaps he may not object to the following remark as corroborative of his discovery: *cheff* in French has the meaning of "fag-end of a piece of cloth," and *chiffe* is a "paltry cloth or rag." The origin and meaning of the word *sheaf* may probably be found in an old French dictionary.

But as there are spots in the sun, Mr. Staunton, I presume, has committed an oversight in his reading of "it lifted up *his* head," instead of *its* head; *Hamlet,* act first, scene second. In the quarto of 1603, to which he refers, we read :—

"And lifted up his head to motion,
Like as *he* would speak."

Pem. "If what in rest you have, in right you hold,"—

King John, act iv., scene 2.

This passage has caused much discussion; may not *in right* be a misprint for *unright?*

Brut. " For if thou path, thy native semblance on,"—
Julius Cæsar, act ii., scene 1.

Another contested passage; may not *path* be a misprint for *pass*?

" O, it came o'er my ear like the sweet sound,
That breathes upon a bank of violets,
Stealing and giving odour."—
Twelfth Night, act i., scene 1.

"So the early text," says Mr. Staunton, "but Pope changed *sound* to *south*, and the alteration has been approved, perhaps too readily, by nearly every editor since his time." Mr. Knight, I think, adopts the same reading, and has given other reasons than those adduced by Mr. Staunton, why *south* could not have been the word used by Shakspere. Both editors, I believe, are correct in rejecting *south*; but I never heard of a *sound* "stealing and giving odour;" the image is too incongruous, although a sound breathing is unobjectionable. *Sound* is merely a misprint for *wind*, and the "sweet wind" is the Zephyr,* which "is said to produce flowers and fruits by the sweetness of its breath." How the poor ignorant Shakspere would have been belaboured by the classical Popes, Johnsons, and Farmers, had the misprint in the early text been *south*, for then they might have discovered, "the breath of Auster is pernicious to flowers."

---

* " Mild as when Zephyrus on Flora breathes."—*Milton.*

Since writing the above, I find Rowe changed *sound* into *wind*, meaning, it must be presumed, the south wind; but the following lines appear to settle the question:—

Bel.   " O thou goddess,
Thou divine Nature, how thyself thou blazon'st
In these two princely boys! They are as gentle
As zephyrs, blowing below the violet,
Not wagging his sweet head."
Sooth. I saw Jove's bird, the Roman eagle, wing'd
From the spungy south to this part of the west."—
Cymbeline, act iv., scene 2.

Mr. Halliwell in his edition of *Marston*, appears to have misapprehended the following passage:—

Ant. "The first thing he spake was,—Mellida!
And then he swooned.
Mel. Aye me!
Ant. Why sigh you, fair?
Ros. Nothing but little humours; good sweet, on.—
Antonio and Mellida, p. 16.

In a note, the editor observes,—" *Ros.* This prefix should obviously be *Mel.*;" but that it is the lively Rosaline, and not the gentle Mellida, who pertly replies to Antonio dressed as an Amazon, may be judged from the last line in the scene:—

Ros. " Sweet Lady, nay *good sweet*, now by my troth weelc be bedfellows."

" O thou allbearing earth;"—" O chaune thy breast."
Act iii., p. 31.

instead of "*O chaune,*" Mr. Dilke reads,—"*Open thy breast.*" But *chaune* is merely a misprint for *cleave*;—and "wound the earth that it may *cleave* in twain," says Tamburlaine.

On entering upon this inquiry I commenced, as already stated, with *Romeo and Juliet;* I then read *Hamlet,* being the next play in the same volume of the *Pictorial Shakspere;* and not having seen either of the plays for more than twenty years, I was forcibly struck, however paradoxical it may sound, with the similarity of character in *Romeo and Hamlet;* that is, as far as the elements are concerned. Romeo is gentleness with resolution, a keen wit, a little more impulsive, but then he is younger, under a southern sky, and his disease is love; whilst Hamlet's simulated madness necessitates an increased watchfulness over his impulses.

In two plays so dissimilar and representing two so dissimilar phases of the mind, parallel passages are not likely to occur; but we may compare Hamlet's state of mind after the interview with his father's spirit, and Romeo's on hearing of the death of Juliet :—

Hor. " These are but wild and hurling words, my lord,
Ham. It is an honest ghost.
  You hear this fellow in the cellarage.
  Well said, old mole! can'st work i' the ground
    so fast."—*Hamlet,* act i., scene 5.
Bal. " Your looks are pale and wild.
Rom. Tush, thou art deceived.

Death, lie thou there, by a dead man interr'd.
How oft when men are at the point of death
Have they been merry."—*Romeo and Juliet*, act v.

The cast of thought in these passages is evidently similar; the difference lies in time and circumstance; both Romeo and Hamlet give vent to their overwrought feelings in bitter jests. The behaviour of Hamlet to Laertes, is throughout identical with Romeo's behaviour to Tybalt and Paris. "The wit of Romeo," says Mr. Knight, "is the unaccustomed play of the intellect, when the passions have come to the clenching point,— but it is under control;" "the courage of Romeo is reflective and forbearing;" assuredly Hamlet's courage is also reflective and forbearing; and his wit is certainly under control.

The resemblance is much stronger, and the divergence far less in the first sketch, than in the perfect Hamlet. "Mr. Hallam, speaking of *Romeo and Juliet* as an early production of our poet, points out as a proof of this, 'the want of that thoughtful philosophy, which, when once it had germinated in Shakspere's mind, never ceased to display itself.' *Hamlet*, as it now stands, is full of this thoughtful philosophy. But the original sketch, as given in the quarto of 1603, exhibits few traces of it in the form of didactic observations. The whole dramatic conduct of the action is indeed demonstrative of a philosophical conception of incidents and characters: but in the form to which Mr. Hallam refers, 'the thoughtful philosophy' is almost entirely wanting in that sketch."—*Pictorial Shakspere*.

That Hamlet is Shakspere himself ought only to be

mentioned, to be granted;—the philosophical soliloquies, the reflections in the churchyard, are acknowledged to be his own meditations; the wit is essentially that of the hero of the *Mermaid*; the remarks about the play are acknowledged to be his; the advice to the players evidently his own opinions, in fact himself speaking; and the quarrel with his friends has been before alluded to;—take away then the witty sallies, the philosophy, the scenes with the players and his friends, and what remains of *Hamlet* but the scene with the ghost and the soliloquy about his mother, which is the very passage that forced on me the conviction, Hamlet is Shakspere himself, and not, strickly speaking, a poetical conception, for the soliloquy is in tone and feeling identical with various sonnets.

With regard to the passage, "for the play, I remember, pleased not the million," Mr. Knight observes, "the introduction of these lines, we think, cannot be accounted for upon any other supposition, but that they were written by Shakspere himself; and he is so thoroughly in earnest in his criticism upon the play, and his complaint of its want of success is so apparently sincere, that it is impossible to imagine, that the passage had reference to something non-existent." And I may add, the passage about "his two school-fellows" at the end of the third act, grated so harshly on my feelings, that I felt Shakspere must have had a quarrel with two of his friends.

Further, I may remark, that Hamlet and Shakspere are of the same age. Hamlet is usualy spoken of as being a very young man; but it seems highly improbable, imcompatible with the character, that a man so well acquainted, so versed in the ways of the world, should only "*have just crossed the threshold of manhood;*" and under the persuasion, that in its composition Shakspere had drawn his materials from the burning fiery lava of his own feelings, the genuine potheen of life, instead of having his muse inspired by the cold mountain dew of Parnassus or by the watery springs of Helicon; under this impression, I have examined and compared certain dates in the play, in reference to Shakspere's own age and that of his parents.

John Shakspere is supposed to have been born about 1530, and he married Mary Arden, in December, 1557, consequently when the play was written in 1588, it could be justly said of them:—

> " Full thirty times hath Phœbus' cart gone round
> Neptune's salt-wash and Tellus' orbed ground;
> And thirty dozen moons with borrow'd sheen,
> About the world have times twelve thirties been;
> Since love our hearts, and *Hymen did our hands*,
> Unite commutual in most sacred bands."

and the clown says, "I have been sexton here, man and boy, thirty years;" the coincidence in the years is at least curious. Again the clown says, he has been a grave-maker ever since "the very day that young Hamlet was born;" the clown refers to his appointment, of course he was not the grave-maker when a boy;—and again he says, "Here's a scull now: this scull has lain in the earth three-and-twenty years." "Alas, poor Yorick!" says Hamlet, "I knew him, Horatio." Now the grave-digger could scarcely have called him young

Hamlet, had he been thirty years of age; altho' he might have been called young, longer than usual, in contradistinction to old Hamlet, his father. Shakspere appears, like De Quincey, to have remembered some old servant or friend of the family when he was only eighteen or twenty months old.

The deliberate and precise alteration of the various dates in the amended copy, clearly and decisively points out Shakspere's intention.

Consequently there can be no doubt, the buried Majesty of Denmark was in the poet's mind his own father; and the Queen? of all his female creations the most poetical,—of all, the most practical, high-spirited, and affectionate, dotingly fond of her son, and as much doted upon by the living as by her former husband;— who can this wonderful woman be? Who else but his own mother, Mary Arden, the poetical and practical mother of the poetical and practical son.

One problem, which it is supposed Shakspere has undertaken to solve in this play, is, that the madness, under which Hamlet appears to be labouring, is in reality assumed; essentially a medico-psychological study; has he succeeded in carrying out this idea? Apparently not; for tho' it is in a measure spoken of as a disputed point, yet, commentators and critics of the highest authority assert, he is not perfectly sane. "Mr. Kean's conception of the part was good, the melancholy abstraction, the vacillation, the derangement of a noble mind o'erthrown, partly affected and partly real, were finely delineated."—*Life of Charles Kean*, p. 260.

This question is not to be settled by eloquent periods and ornate descriptions, but by an analysis or anatomical dissection of the play: for we have to deal with a young doctor, who had intimately studied the divine architecture of man, whatever may have been his knowledge of the "Architecture of the Heavens," at that time a disputed point.

The play opens with a scene proving the reality of the ghost. In the second scene Hamlet makes his appearance quibbling; from which it may be inferred, he is not only witty, but naturally of a cheerful disposition. In his reply to his mother, like a tender and affectionate son, he avoids wounding her feelings; but in the first copy we read:—

"Him have I lost, I must *of course* forego,"

a line clearly showing his grief depended not on the loss of his father; but as such an observation might raise in his mother's mind a suspicion her marriage was the cause, the poet in the amended copy judiciously omitted the line and put in its stead:—

"But I have that within which passeth show."

No sooner is Hamlet left alone, than he gives vent to his feelings in a speech of the most exquisite sensibility and pathos, concluding with:—

"O most wicked speed, to post
With such dexterity to incestuous sheets;
It is not, nor it cannot come to good;
But break, my heart; for I must hold my tongue!"

Yet the critics and commentators, apparently resolved in the very beginning to make him a weak-minded man, unanimously attribute his melancholy to the death of his father, although in the whole speech there is not the slightest expression of regret for his loss; the real cause being the deep wound to his moral and religious feelings, that his mother, whom he so dearly loved, that such a radiant angel should have *sinned*, married her deceased husband's brother. No doubt Hamlet has a natural regret for the loss of his father; but he would rather, he himself had died, than his mother should have committed such a fearful sin, an incestuous marriage :—

> " Would I had met my dearest foe in heaven,
>   Ere I had seen that day, Horatio."

This scene reminds us of the first scene in *All's Well that End's Well*, written in the preceding year, 1587; in each instance there is a mystification, which is cleared up to the audience by a soliloquy.

The King and Queen and all the Court suppose, Hamlet's grief proceeds from the loss of his father; nor does he, because he dare not undeceive them :—

> " But break, my heart! for I must hold my tongue."

It is comfortable to have an authority on one's side; Professor Richardson in his *Philosophical Analysis of Shakspere's Remarkable Characters*, thus writes,—" the death of his father was a natural evil, and as such he endures it. The impropriety of Gertrude's behaviour, her ingratitude to the memory of her former husband, and the depravity she discovers in the choice of a successor, afflict his soul, and cast him into utter agony. Here then is the principle and spring of all his actions."

In the third scene we have another insight into Hamlet's character, which has apparently been quite overlooked by the critics:—

Laer.   " Farewell.   [*exit* Laertes.
Pol.   What is 't, Ophelia, he hath said to you?
Oph.   So please you, something touching the lord Hamlet.
Pol.   Marry, well bethought:
         'Tis told me, he hath *very oft of late*
         Given private time to you; and you yourself
         Have of your audience been most free and bounteous.
Oph.   He hath, my lord, of late, made many tenders
         Of his affection to me.
Pol.   Affection? puh! you speak like a green girl,
         Unsifted in such perilous circumstance.
Oph.   My lord, he hath importun'd me with love,
         In honourable fashion.
Pol.   Ay, fashion you may call it; go to, go to.
Oph.   And hath given countenance to his speech, my lord,
         With all the vows of heaven.
Pol.   Ay, springes to catch woodcocks.
                  This is for all,—
         I would not, in plain terms, *from this time* forth,
         Have you to slander any moment's leisure,
         As to give words or talk with the lord Hamlet.
         Look to 't, I charge you; come your ways.
Oph.   I shall obey, my lord."—Act i., scene 3.

Here it is evident, Hamlet has, like Helena in *All's Well that Ends Well*, " very oft of late " *forgotten his father* and is making hot love to Ophelia;—we may then sum up,—in the audience chamber Hamlet makes his appearance quibbling, consequently he cannot be in a very melancholy mood, but in his address to his mother and in the soliloquy, he shows us the exquisite sensibility of his nature, and how deeply distressed and outraged have been his moral and religious sentiments, by his mother's marriage;—he receives his friends graciously; and common report says, he gives much of his time to Ophelia. I trust then, it has been clearly proved, Hamlet is not at the opening of the play the profoundly melancholy character he is generally represented.

Throughout the interview with the ghost, Hamlet's intellect remains clear and unaffected; he never loses his presence of mind; the frenzied excitement he felt at first, gradually softens down during the spirit's narrative, giving place to a desire of revenge. By the fading away of the ghost, the strain on his nerves and intellect is somewhat relieved, and he recovers still further *by the act of writing* in his tables; so that on the arrival of his friends he seeks to turn off their inquiries and give relief to his still agitated feelings by jesting; and it is possible, this excitement of the feelings, with intellectual power to control them, may have suggested the idea of feigning himself mad.

Before proceeding any further, we must examine into the duration or period of time occupied by the play; for there is no immediate connexion marked between the first and second acts; but as the second act opens with Polonius sending money and notes to his son, a considerable period must have elapsed since Laertes departed, and since Hamlet saw the ghost.

The first act occupied two nights and the intervening day. In the second act, scene first, Polonius has just dismissed Reynaldo, when the gentle Ophelia hurries in with her hand on her heart, "Oh, my lord, I have been so affrighted," and tells him about Hamlet's strange visitation; Polonius then goes to the castle, "come go we to the king," to whom he immediately announces:—

> "The ambassadors from Norway, my good lord,
> Are joyfully returned;"—Act ii., scene 2.

on leaving the royal presence, or rather *exeunt* king and attendants, he has an amusing conversation with Hamlet, to whom he presents Rosencrantz and Guildenstern. We have then the scene with the players, in which Hamlet says, "we'll have 't tomorrow night;" the act terminates with the soliloquy "the spirit that I have seen may be the devil, the play's the thing, wherein I'll catch the conscience of the king."

We thus see the second act occupies exactly one day.

On the following day in the evening, the play is performed; thus the whole of the third act, and the first three scenes of the fourth act occupy one day and a night; and to Hamlet's remark, "my father died within these two hours," Ophelia replies, "Nay, 'tis twice two months, my lord;" and as the first act occurred two months after the death of the king, "But two months dead!—nay, not so much, not two," consequently *two months must have elapsed between the first and second acts.*

The fourth scene in the fourth act occurs at daybreak, and the three remaining scenes occupy at least several weeks, as Fortinbras and the English ambassadors appear in the last act.

The fifth act occupies half a day or a few hours only, as the king on leaving the churchyard says to Laertes, "we'll put the matter to the present push."

We may now return and examine Hamlet's conduct in act second, scene first. For two long months had Hamlet submitted to have his letters refused, and access to his Ophelia denied; what! what! I hear voices around me exclaiming, Hamlet constantly breaking his vow! impossible! it is, however, ye impalpable beings! perfectly true, down in black and white, on the word of Ophelia. Polonius laid his commands on her at the very hour Horatio was telling Hamlet about the ghost; we may be certain, he neither visited nor wrote to her that evening; consequently it must have been during these two months, after he had vowed his vow, "unmixed with baser matter," that Ophelia "did repel his letters and denied his access." But when has Shakspere ever made love "baser matter," "seconds;" love is the creative principle of nature, and the poet of nature has always made lovely woman the *primum mobile;* Silvia, Juliet, &c., all quit father and mother and make runaway matches, and are by the moral poet of nature punished or rewarded according to their deserts.

The truth then must be faced; Hamlet is undeniably in an ecstasy of love, as Polonius calls it; and no doubt the interview was followed by beneficial effects on both sides; his anxiety would be relieved by the sight of her; and Ophelia? less palpitation of the heart, less sighing over her "sewing in her chamber;" she now would have undoubted evidence, that his *affection* depended on her love, was caused by her unkindness. And I have noticed it these thirty years, young ladies do not break their hearts, though their cruelty may drive their lovers to distraction; they seem, sweet enchantresses, to have an implicit reliance on certain charms in their possession to cure the disease; was such Shakspere's opinion? how was Ophelia affected on this occasion, and also the Queen?—

Pol. "How now, Ophelia? what's the matter?
Oph. Alas, my lord, I have been so affrighted.
Pol. Mad for thy love?
Oph.   My lord, I do not know;
But truly I do fear it."—Act ii., scene 1.

Queen. "And for your part, Ophelia, I do wish,
That your good beauties be the happy cause
Of Hamlet's wildness: so shall I hope your virtues
Will bring him to his wonted way again,
To both your honours.
Oph.   Madam, I wish it may."
     Act. iii., scene 1.

O, sweet, innocent, and gentle Ophelia! the faith of the sisterhood is strong within thee. On the supposition that *only a few days elapse* between the first and second acts, this scene has generally been regarded as a simulated ecstasy on the part of Hamlet, to deceive the king and his courtiers; but the lapse of two months, with the rejection of his letters and visits, incontestably settles the question. This view of his passionate love is confirmed by his own self-accusing conscience in the Queen's bedchamber:—

Ham. "Do you not come your tardy son to chide,
That, laps'd in time and passion, let's go by
The important acting of your dread command?"

On the following morning, Hamlet having been summoned to the presence of the king, meets Ophelia; at this interview Ophelia, discovering he is more seriously affected than she had previously imagined, becomes herself deeply agitated and distressed; and soon after, hearing of her father's lamentable death and her lover's banishment, her brother being still in Paris, no wonder the young lady breaks her heart and becomes deranged.

On the same evening, after this meeting with Ophelia, the play is performed, at which the king is proved guilty;—soon afterwards, Hamlet, just on the point of departure to visit the queen, thus expresses his burning desire for vengeance:—

> "Now could I drink hot blood,
> And do such bitter business as the day
> Would quake to look on."

On the way to his mother he suddenly comes on the king at his prayers; notwithstanding the privacy and secrecy of the opportunity, by a desperate effort of his will he controls the almost irresistible impulse to kill him; strange to say, this scene is regarded as a proof of his irresolution; and though Johnson accused him of being influenced by motives inhuman and fiendish, it is now universally agreed, the reasons assigned by Hamlet are not his real motives, but mere excuses, a self-deception, to avoid the shedding of blood, marks of irresolution and procrastination. The critics in accusing him on this occasion of weakness and irresolution, are certainly consistent with their previous opinion in attributing his deep grief to the death of his father, though he never uttered a single regret for him, nor said a word about him except that he was "an excellent king," and compared with his brother, "Hyperion to a satyr."

Hamlet, like his critics, is consistent with himself; the very next night, being at sea, he writes out a new commission:—

> *Ham.* "An earnest conjuration from the king,—
> As England was his faithful tributary, &c.,
> Without debatement further, more, or less,
> He should the bearers *put to sudden death,*
> *Not shriving time allowed.*"

It would seem, these erroneous impressions about Hamlet's character, have arisen from a misapprehension or inattention to the doctrines of his religion;—a heart full of tenderness and noble feelings, a keen and ready wit, quick in action as thought or lightning, with a will strong to control the most sudden and violent impulse, an intellect godlike, but *subordinate to his religious belief.* Had he killed the king at his prayers, his soul at the moment pure and free from sin, what would have been *the inevitable consequence?* Scarcely could he have sheathed his sword, 'ere his father's ghost appears, furious, "poor fool! weak, rash, and imbecile fool! you swore to *revenge* my murder; your uncle is in heaven and I'm in hell;" *exit* the perturbed spirit; Hamlet, now really mad, rushes after his father to the regions below;—finale, an awful smell of brimstone.

His father's spirit had told him something about the other world:—

> *Ghost.* "I am thy father's spirit;
> Doom'd for a certain term to walk the night;
> And, for the day, confin'd to fast in fires,
> Till the foul crimes, done in my days of nature
> Are burnt and purg'd away."

Shakspere is not answerable for the religion in the play, which is the Roman Catholic; and probably purgatory was still in his day the popular belief amongst the lower classes. "Purgatory, a place in which souls are supposed by the Papists to be purged by fire from carnal impurities, before they are received into heaven."—*Johnson*.

Hamlet therefore naturally wishes his father's murderer to undergo the penalty of his crime, *a limited period* of punishment, and not an eternal damnation. The following passage has evidently been misunderstood as well by Johnson as by the Coleridges and Lambs:—

> *Ham.* "Then trip him, that his heels may kick at heaven;
> And that his soul may be as damn'd and black,
> As hell, whereto it goes."

"*hell*" here does not mean the place of eternal punishment; but purgatory, or the place of departed spirits; *vide Johnson*:—

> "the place of separate souls whether good or bad.

and in *Tamburlaine*, Cosroe exclaims:—

> "My soul begins to take her flight to hell,
> And summons all my senses to depart."

and in Nash's *Pierce Pennilesse*, his Supplication to the Devil, we read, p. 66,—"Hell is a place where the souls of intemperate men, and ill livers of all sorts, are detained and imprisoned till the general resurrection."

The last words of the ghost were, "remember me;" that is, not his mere murder, but *his suffering the tortures of purgatory*; Claudius must therefore undergo the same penalties: but the critics can not or will not perceive the difference between temporal and eternal punishment; they will persist in judging Hamlet by protestant doctrines and not as a papist. Shakspere avoids the abusive language of the early reformers, and generally portrays his friars as good and estimable men; but he never hesitates to point out at the same time the evil tendencies of the doctrines of the Church of Rome; and his intention on the present occasion evidently is, to show the injurious action of a belief in purgatory; how much it tends to nourish an unforgiving spirit; just as in the *Lucrece* he shows the injurious effects of the priestly power of absolution; when Tarquin has his hand on the chamber-door, he starts, frightened at the thought of his *intended* crime, but is *instantly re-assured*:

"Then Love and Fortune be my gods, my guide!
My will is back'd with resolution;
Thoughts are but dreams till their effects be tried,
The blackest sin is clear'd with absolution."—
Stanza 51.

Hamlet's revenge must consequently be regarded as essentially papistical, and perfectly natural under the circumstances.

On quitting the king he proceeds to his mother's chamber; after a few words, hearing a noise behind the arras, quick as lightning, he draws his sword, "a rat, dead for a ducat, dead;" unfortunately, instead of the king, it was that "wretched, rash, intruding fool," Polonius. To his affrighted exclamation on the sudden entrance of the ghost, his mother sighs forth, "Alas he's mad;" of course she listens patiently, like a sensible woman, not understanding a word about it, to his learned dissertation on insanity; nods yes, yes, to everything he says, and departs promising him, "I have no life to breathe what thou hast said to me;" and goes, like an innocent and affectionate wife straight to her jolly old king and tells him all, "poor dear boy! alas, he's mad." The queen never had, and even now, she has not the slightest suspicion the king had killed his brother; nor had Hamlet the slightest suspicion of such a deed, till Horatio told him about the ghost:—

Ham. "My father's spirit in arms! all is not well;
I doubt some foul play."

and on the spirit telling him of his murder, he exclaims in astonishment, "Murther?"

As the ghost, on this occasion, in the queen's bed-chamber, is pleased to remark:—

"Do not forget; this visitation
Is but to whet thy almost blunted purpose,"

the commentators have eagerly seized upon this unlucky observation, as undoubted proof, on the word of a ghost, of Hamlet's irresolution and unfixedness of purpose; but they have merely dropped on a mare's nest! every child in the kingdom knows, a ghost knows nothing except just what concerns himself; and this ghost, as Shakspere intended, betrays the most astonishing ignorance; for he says, "I am come to whet thy almost blunted purpose;" and yet Hamlet has just slain Polonius; the ghost knew from his cold midnight walks, and from not seeing his fraternal murderer by the fireside below, that Hamlet had not yet revenged his murder; he therefore naturally supposed his son had been remiss in the undertaking. But the fact is, Hamlet, being a moral and religious man, and fearing lest the spirit might have been an evil spirit tempting him to sin, would not put his uncle to death, till he had clearer evidence of his guilt; which was proved only an hour or two ago, and from that moment his blood had been boiling at fever-heat to execute his father's dread command; with a desperate effort he had *luckily* checked the violent impulse to kill the king at his prayers, and then, with thought rapid as lightning, and with a will as quick and decisive, he passed his sword through the arras, thinking the king was there; assuredly Hamlet needed no fresh stimulus; evidently the ghost was at fault; the old gentleman had neglected applying at the telegraph office before leaving home to take his midnight walk.

Hamlet, shortly after his mother's departure, *as may be easily guessed,* was arrested by his two dear friends and taken before the king; who immediately ordered him to sea; on the road to the vessel he soliloquizes:—

" Now whether it be
Bestial oblivion, or some craven scruple
Of thinking too precisely on the event, &c."

This speech has again been adduced as proof of his irresolution and procrastination; but surely it is nothing else than the natural depression following over-excitement; he has not had a wink of sleep for at least twenty-four hours, and during the last twelve his mind has been constantly on the stretch in a state of violent excitement; now that all hope of revenge is over for the present, a depression follows, a hopeless sinking at the heart, though he struggles against it and upbraids himself for not having done, *what he never had an opportunity of doing;*

he now blames himself for ever having doubted the spirit was his father's; but a few hours' sleep on board the vessel restored life and energy to his exhausted frame.

We next meet with Hamlet in the church-yard; as the funeral procession approaches, he notices:—

> "The queen, the courtiers: Who is that they follow?
> And with such maimed rites! This doth betoken,
> The corse they follow did with desperate hand
> Foredo its own life. 'Twas of some estate:
> Couch we a while, and mark."

He then overhears Laertes say:—

> "I tell thee, churlish priest,
> A ministering angel shall my sister be,
> When thou liest howling."

Let us remember, that Hamlet has not heard anything of Ophelia since last he saw her in the palace, we may then judge, what an intensity of passion and self-control must be concentrated in these words, "What, the fair Ophelia!* On Laertes leaping into the grave and giving way to the violence of his feelings, is it wonderful or surprising, that Hamlet's pent-up feelings should burst out beyond all control, and sweep him away in the torrent? and yet, what? he leaps into the grave, is assaulted by Laertes, and this so-called madman says:—

> "I prithee, take thy fingers from my throat;
> Sir, though I am not splenetive and rash,
> Yet have I something in me dangerous,
> Which let thy wiseness fear: Away thy hand."

The very language of one exerting the highest mastery

---

* Romeo's exclamation, on hearing of the death of Juliet, "Is it even so?" is identical with Hamlet's; each has the same powerful will to suppress any sudden emotion.

over himself; they are separated, and Hamlet makes a passionate speech, which is neither a real aberration nor a simulated frenzy, but merely the speech of a man in a towering passion, ending, "Nay, an thou'lt mouth, I'll rant as well as thou;" the queen echoes the cry, "this is mere madness;" and then Hamlet makes a most characteristic speech; the first half, the quiet observation of a man who has completely recovered from his passion; the second half, simulated madness on purpose to carry on the deception about his lunacy:—

Ham.   "Hear you, sir;
What is the reason you use me thus?
I lov'd you ever: But it is no matter;
Let Hercules himself do what he may,
The cat will mew, and dog will have his day."

That the king and queen should attribute Hamlet's conduct to insanity is natural enough; but if either be mad, Laertes is the one; there has been time enough for his grief to settle down, and yet he leaps into the grave, calling frantically out:—

"Now pile your dust upon the quick and dead;
Till of this flat a mountain you have made,
To o'er-top old Pelion, or the skyish head
Of blue Olympus."

But in defence of his sanity, it must be remembered, this speech is undoubtedly a satirical stroke of the poet against the affectation of "the young gentlemen of the two Universities," and of his poetical rivals, Peele, Greene, and Marlowe, who could only express the violence of their love and grief by such bombastic raving; and to which Hamlet replies:—

> "And, if thou prate of mountains, let them throw
> Millions of acres on us; till our ground,
> Singeing his pate against the burning zone,
> Make Ossa like a wart!"

not a very irrational reply for a man in a passion.

After returning from the funeral, Horatio says:—

> "It must be shortly known to him from England,
> What is the issue of the business there.
>
> *Ham.* It will be short; the interim is mine;
> And a man's life's no more than to say, one."

It is folly guessing and scheming what Hamlet would or might have done; it is clear he intended acting quickly and decisively; but events were hurrying on with fearful rapidity beyond the control of the actors; for scarcely had he told Horatio, how cleverly he had paid off Rosencrantz and Guildenstern, when Lord Osric comes with a message from the king requesting him to play at foils with Laertes; he accepts the chalenge; and to Horatio's remark, "you will lose this wager, my lord," he replies, "I do not think so; but thou wouldst not think, how ill all's here about my heart; but it is no matter." How could he feel otherwise than ill at heart? it is not more than an hour or two, since he first heard of Ophelia's death, saw her buried with maimed rites, and quarrelled with her brother, whom he had "ever loved;" he cannot, like Romeo, say, "I'll lie with her to-night;" he must fulfil the dread command of his father's spirit; and when executed, what is the world to him? Ophelia dead! Ophelia whom he loved more than forty thousand brothers, and for whose love he wept over the dead body of Polonius, "he weeps for what is done." In this state of depression, and the heart ill at ease, the mind naturally anticipates coming evils, and is more inclined to trust to chance or fate, than rely on its own energies; but Hamlet rises superior to this feeling, and is, throughout, thoroughly master of himself; in the scene with the frivolous courtier he is "most acute, playful, but always the gentleman;" and, as he quibbled at his first appearance, he again in this last scene, notwithstanding his being so ill at heart, shows the witty and poetical side of his nature:—

> *Ham.* "I'll be your foil, Laertes; in mine ignorance
> Your skill shall, like a star, i' the darkest night,
> Stick fiery off indeed."

And on hearing the weapon was poisoned, he instantly stabs the king, "now venom do thy work," and makes the horror-stricken wretch drink of the poisoned bowl; he acts with the same rapid thought and decisive will, as when he pierced the arras with his sword, "a rat, dead for a ducat, dead;" and thus the king dies at the culminating point of his iniquitous career.

"The catastrophe," says Johnson, "is not very happily produced; the exchange of weapons is rather an expedient of necessity than a stroke of art. A scheme might easily be formed to kill Hamlet with the dagger, and Laertes with the bowl." Let us examine and analyse this scene of horrors.—The Queen fallen from her original loveliness and purity, and become addicted to drink, dies of the bowl poisoned by him, who first poisoned her mind, corrupted her affections from her husband, and induced her to form an incestuous marriage; she dies first, mercifully. The king dies at the moment, his cup of guilt is full to the brim; his beloved Gertrude dying by his guilty means, and he not daring to put forth a hand to save her. Laertes was guilty in the first instance of casting suspicion on Hamlet's honour and love, and now like a base knight he fights with a poisoned foil, and justly falls by the hand of Hamlet. The only innocent person is Hamlet, but tragic propriety compels his death; he has however the consolation of having revenged his father's murder; nor could he have died more appropriately than by Laertes' hand, whose father he had killed, though accidentally; and of whose sister's insanity and death he was the unhappy, though innocent cause. We thus see, what a botch Johnson with his bowl and dagger would have made of the retributive justice, so clearly shown in this last scene.

Putting Hamlet himself aside, it becomes a curious question, What was Shakspere's intention in writing this fifth act? it is a satire throughout; the scene with Osric is acknowledged to be a satire, so is the scene with the clowns; and by like reasoning, the burial scene is a satire on the forms and ceremonies of the Romish Church; the bombast of Laertes is in the same category; and when Hamlet leaps into the grave, calling out, "I am Hamlet the Dane," had not Laertes acted naturally, and violently assaulted him, what a fine opportunity for the poet to have given us a poetical duet in alternate chaunts to the praise of Ophelia; particularly as Hamlet, overpowered by his love, forgets on this occasion his pretended lunacy—forgets the ghost and the dread command, "remember me;" but was not Hamlet's excited harangue also intended for satire, especially in ridicule of *Tamburlaine's* rhodomontade when Zenocrate dies :—

"*What, is she dead?* Tchelles, draw thy sword
And wound the earth, that it may cleave in twain,"

the exclamation, "What, the fair Ophelia," appears to be the link connecting the two scenes together :—

"Nay, an' thou'lt mouth,
I'll rant as well as thou;"

it should be remembered, *Tamburlaine* at this time was a popular drama; nor is it credible Shakspere would have placed Hamlet in such a false position, as the hero of a disgraceful row at Ophelia's grave, without some definite object, readily understood by the audience; the poet has therefore given us in its prosaic truthfulness to nature, a scene both local and universal in its application, a satire against Elizabethan bombast and the sentimental prettinesses of the classical school.

Thus while these various scenes of buffoonery for the million, and of Night Thoughts for a Young, are woven together into an harmonious whole, Hamlet throughout, except at the duel, may be regarded as the mere puppet of the poet, a mouthpiece for the expression of his own sentiments; hence the supposition, which the soliloquy in act first, scene second, gave rise to, is most forcibly and wonderfully confirmed, and becomes a conviction in this fifth and final act,—that Hamlet is Shakspere himself.

Here follow a few remarks on some of the much vexed passages:—

 King. "But now my cousin Hamlet, and my son,—
 Ham. A little more than kin and less than kind." [*aside.*
           Act i., scene 2.

"*less than kind*" is usually explained by "I am little of the same *nature* with you;" this explanation, however, conveys an unfavourable impression, as a vain and conceited remark, and uncalled for, especially as an *aside;* as if Hamlet had said, "I am not such a vile fellow as you;" whereas, the straightforward meaning, "Altho' I am now more nearly related to you, my feelings are less than kind," shows to the audience the exact state of his sentiments at the moment. The quibble may then, perhaps, be thus explained, "A little more than kin and less than *natural,*" that is, "Altho' I am now, in a sense, your son, I have not the natural feelings of a son towards you."

 King. "How is it that the clouds still hang on you?
 Ham. Not so, my lord; I am too much i' the sun."—
           Act. i., scene 2.

"*too much i' the sun*" is usually explained as meaning, "deprived of the charities of kindred." Mr. Staunton's annotation is, "By this Hamlet may mean, 'I am too much in the way,' a mote in the royal eye; but his reply is purposely enigmatical."

The observation, "less than kind," was an *aside;* but

"too much i' the sun," is a direct and open reply to his majesty; it must therefore bear a courteous and even complimentary signification; as if Hamlet had said, "Not so, my lord, I am too much in your Majesty's favour; you are too gracious for me to feel myself under a cloud." To be in disgrace at Court is to be under a cloud; to be in favour is to be basking in the sunshine of the royal presence, one of the commonest images in the language. This explanation is confirmed by the concluding words of the scene, and by the following extract:—"The Queene seemade troubled to-daye, says Harrington. Hatton came out from her presence with ill countenance, and pulled me aside by the girdle, and saide, in secret waie, If you have any suite to daie, I praye you put it aside. *The sunne doth not shine.*"—Drake's *Shakspere*, vol. ii., p. 150.

This harsh explanation, "deprived of the charities of kindred," reminds us of "the swaggering upspring reels," which does not mean "*the upstart king,*" but a dance, a kind of hop; and thus through these erroneous interpretations, there is attributed to Hamlet a worse feeling towards his uncle at the present moment, than the context justifies.

Ham. [*reads*] "For if the sun breed maggots in a dead dog, being a god kissing carrion,—Have you a daughter?"—
Act ii., scene 2.

This passage has caused much ingenious speculation; but the simplest and easiest explanation is, not unfrequently, nearer the truth than a more erudite or far-fetched meaning. Instead of finishing the sentence, Hamlet carries on his joke of pretending not to know Polonius, and asks, "Have you a daughter?" On this occasion we must remember, the conversation is a *tête-à-tête*, and that two months have passed away since Hamlet saw the ghost; time has weakened the impression, he suspects it to have been an illusion, though at intervals the idea rises vividly in his mind, it may have been his father's spirit; in the meantime absence has added strength to his love, by dwelling on the image of Ophelia; and it is hardly two hours ago since he was made supremely happy by a stolen interview with her:—his asking, "Have you a daughter?" is therefore a direct allusion to his visit that morning, and to the strict seclusion in which she had been kept during the last two months, not allowed to walk out, lest Hamlet should meet her. He therefore says, "Let her not walk i' the sun: conception is a blessing; but not as your daughter may conceive,—[*before marriage*] friend, look to 't." This mocking or jesting should be compared with Polonius' speech to Ophelia, to which it is the retort courteous.—

> *Pol.* Affection? puh! you speak like a green girl,
> Unsifted in such perilous circumstance.
> Do not believe his vows,
> Mere implorators of unholy suits,
> Breathing like sanctified and pious bonds,
> The better to beguile."—
>
> Act i., scene 3.

"Soft you now!
The fair Ophelia."—
Act iii., scene 1.

With regard to the soliloquy, "To be or not to be," Mr. Hunter in his *Illustrations* has drawn attention to the fact, that in the first sketch the king says, "See where he comes poring upon a book," and he adds, "It is thus manifest the poet's intention was, that these should be meditations of Hamlet on something which he found written in a book which he holds in his hand, and are not to be regarded as from the beginning thoughts springing up in his own mind."

Before analysing his conduct to Ophelia, we must first carefully examine into all the circumstances respecting the exact position of each party. Ophelia has for two months steadily obeyed her father's injunctions in denying herself to Hamlet: but yesterday he rushed into her presence in an ecstasy of love, and to-day there is a decided change in her favour; the king and queen are consenting parties to her love; as gentleness and submission are two leading traits in her character, she readily agrees to practise what she must regard as a very innocent bit of deception on her lover; she looks forward then to the interview, a little anxious, perhaps, but with feminine faith in her charms. But a great change has come over Hamlet since yesterday morning; this evening will be decided the guilt or innocence of the king; he is therefore absorbed with his vow; love must yield to his father's dread command; on his way to the presence of the king he revolves in his mind a philosophical problem on life and death; he is therefore in a grave and serious mood.

Notwithstanding the deep affection he bore Ophelia, and the serious mood he was in, Shakspere will make him act inexorably according to the laws of his feigned madness; and happily his disease is a melancholy and not a lunacy. All his observations, therefore, are uttered in harmony with his feelings, in a kind, though sad and regretful tone. This view of the question is supported by the remark of the king, "There's something in his soul, o'er which his melancholy *sits on brood,*" words quite incompatible with the supposition he spoke mockingly, dancing and grinning about the lobby like a lunatic.

He first addresses her in words most sweet and sad:—

> "Nymph, in thy orisons,
> Be all my sins remembered."
> "I humbly thank you, well, well, well!"
> "No, no! I never gave you ought."

On her again offering to return his gifts, he then suspects she is playing a part; his "ha! ha!" is simply the exclamation on this suspicion arising in his mind, and he asks, "Are you honest?" merely meaning, "Are you acting honestly, of your own accord, in offering to restore these gifts?" the question is most natural; he had not spoken to her for full two months; she prevaricates of necessity, and says questionly, "My lord!" he is then satisfied she is playing a part, and he quibbles on the word honest, and asks, "Are you fair?" but at the same time everything is done in the kindest and gentlest manner; "Get thee to a nunnery; go thy ways, and quickly too," was the best advice he could give; for this very evening his fate will be decided; "blood and destruction shall be so in use," that her father, the king's confidential minister, had better "let the doors be shut upon him, that he may play the fool nowhere but in's own house." This allusion to her father, which Hamlet certainly could not avoid, as the king and Polonius were listening behind the arras, is the first sentence, and perhaps the only one, that really grated on her feelings; but the young lady got no more than she deserved; she was telling fibs "at home, my lord."

The conversation should be divided into two parts; in the first, Hamlet gives, according to *the method* of his madness, the best possible advice, if she could only have understood it; the latter part is intended to deceive the listeners, and Ophelia of course is not hurt at his remarks, attributing them to his insanity; but the king was a Hamlet also, and not so easily outwitted; his guilty conscience began to suspect that Hamlet's mind was dwelling on his father's sudden death, and "I do doubt the hatch, and the disclose will be some danger." Had Hamlet addressed Ophelia in a jeering and offensive manner, Polonius would certainly have remarked upon it; besides, the king said, "tho' it lacked form a little, it was not like madness." And a few hours after, at the play, he is very attentive, and quite sweet on Ophelia:—

Ham. "No, good mother, here's metal more attractive.
Pol. Oho! do you mark that?"

Ophelia was also probably deceived by Hamlet's mimetic art, "the feature of blown youth, blasted with ecstasy," that is, of melancholia, with its vacant and abstracted look "*bent on vacuity,*" as opposed to the ecstasy of love :—

> "He seem'd to find his way without his eyes;
> And, to the last, *bended their light on me.*"

The grand Anglo-Saxon character of Hamlet, with its sensibilities and energies, is not to be understood by reading his speeches thirty times over as Kemble did, but by a cautious analysis, by comparing passage with passage; throughout this scene, Hamlet acts the melancholic character admirably, *meditative, self-accusing, and suspicious.*

> *Ham.* "When he himself might his quietus make
> With a bare bodkin."—
>
> Act iii., scene 1.

Bodkin is said to be a small sword, and that Cæsar was, according to old writers, slain by bodkins; but Hamlet is speaking slightingly of our tenure of life, "who would bear such fardels, such a weary life, when it can so easily be put an end to by a bodkin, by a little pin;"—a similar passage occurs in *Richard II.* :—

> *K. Rich.* "For within the hollow crown,
> That rounds the mortal temples of a king,
> Keeps death his court: and there the antick sits,
> Scoffing his state, and grinning at his pomp;
> Allowing him a breath, a little scene
> To monarchize, be fear'd, and kill with looks;
> Infusing him with self and vain conceit,—
> As if this flesh, which walls about our life,
> Were brass impregnable, and, humour'd thus,

> Comes at the last, and *with a little pin*
> Bores through his castle wall, and—farewell
> king."—Act iii., scene 2.

The bare bodkin and the little pin should be taken as evidence of Shakspere's anatomical knowledge. His handwriting may also be adduced as evidence of his *medical* profession, at least that he had not been a lawyer's clerk:—

> *Ham.* "I sat me down;
> Devis'd a new commission; wrote it fair;
> *I once did hold it*, as our statists do,
> *A baseness to write fair,* and labour'd much
> How to forget that learning."—Act v., scene 2.

The following passages have been quoted as illustrative of irresolution and weakness in the character of Hamlet:—

1. "But no more like my father
   Than I to Hercules."
2. "The time is out of joint—O cursed spite
   That ever I was born to set it right."
3. Soliloquy after the dismissing the players, act ii.
4. "Now might I do it," &c., act iii., scene 3.
5. Soliloquy, act iv., scene 4.
6. "But thou would'st not think," &c., act v.

The three last passages have been already fully explained. Schlegel says, "But in the resolutions which he so often embraces, and always leaves unexecuted, the weakness of his volition is evident: he does himself only justice when he says, there is no greater dissimilarity than between himself and Hercules."—*Blackwood's Magazine*, vol. xxxvii.

Schlegel is not quite so sane as Hamlet, he confuses self-accusations and reproaches with resolutions.

The germ of Goethe's estimate of Hamlet's character, and of the leading idea which Shakspere intended to convey, is contained in the following paragraph:—

"The time is out of joint; O cursed spite!
That ever I was born to set it right."

"In these words, I imagine, will be found the key to Hamlet's whole procedure. To me it is clear, that Shakspere meant in the present case to represent the effects of a great action laid upon a soul unfit for the performance of it. In this view the whole piece seems to me to be composed."

It is evident, Goethe, like Coleridge, has looked into the depths of his own moral consciousness, and has mistaken his own image for Hamlet; for Goethe had his weak side, "he had only, therefore, to keep in abeyance the native force of resolution, which gave him mastery, and in that abeyance a weak, wavering character stood before him, the original of which was himself."—*Lewes' Life of Goethe.*

Let us now test Goethe's test:—

Ham. "Why what should be the fear?
I do not set my life at a pin's fee;
And, for my soul, what can it do to that,
Being a thing immortal as itself?"

So far he seems to have the soul of a hero, well fitted for the performance of a great action; but two or three hours afterwards, when the excitement has subsided, Shakspere, true to nature, puts into his mouth words denoting exhaustion of body and mind; and showing, if anything further, not weakness, but exquisite sensibility and tenderness. The passage, quoted by Goethe, may be compared with the soliloquy in the fourth act, and also with "how ill all's here about my heart." These three passages occur at a period of depression following violent, and, in two instances, long-continued excitement.

With regard to the soliloquy at the end of the second act, what is Hamlet's position? he has just dismissed the players, and also the two sponges, saying, with the usual courtesy of society, "My good friends, I'll leave you till night: you are welcome to Elsinore."

> *Ros.* "Good my lord!
> *Ham.* Ay, so, God be wi' you."

merely meaning, good riddance of you; has he not just discovered they are false friends, and did he not say, "Nay, then I have an eye of you;" he then breaks out:—

> "O, what a rogue and peasant slave am I!"

uttered in a self-accusing, slightly accented tone; having now the opportunity of testing the king's conscience, he believes for the moment, that his uncle is really guilty, and gradually works himself into a violent passion.

But the first part of this speech is usually delivered in a very different manner;—the reader or actor sits down in an attitude of great exhaustion, and pulling out the white handkerchief, covers his face in due theatrical form; then in a low, depressed, and melancholy tone he drawls out, "O, what a rogue and peasant slave am I!" gradually working himself into a passion on getting to "Am I a coward? who calls me villain?" *De gustibus non disputandum,* every man to his own fancy. But as Hamlet makes his appearance in this scene quizzing Polonius, and becomes moody and suspicious on discovering his two friends to be spies, and on the arrival of the players immediately conceives the idea of testing his uncle's guilt, concealing or keeping down his excitement by again jesting with Polonius, I should suspect, that, on being left alone, he would be in a bitter and scornful, rather than in a low, depressed, and melancholy mood.

I trust it has been clearly proved in the foregoing pages, there are in Hamlet "no tokens of an unhinged mind," no symptoms of an "aberration of intellect;" nor can the passage,—" I have of late, but [wherefore I know not,] lost all my mirth, foregone all custom of exercises," &c., be adduced as evidence of mental alienation. Had this scene, act second, scene second, occurred a few days or within a fortnight after his seeing the ghost, we might suspect, especially as he has just been playing the madman with Polonius, that Hamlet is *simulating* the precursory symptoms of melancholia, the soliloquy at the end being the paroxysm; but as two months have elapsed, such a suspicion is untenable, and he must consequently be regarded as describing his actual condition. It does not, however, follow, that his mind is diseased, since similar symptoms occasionally accompany derangement of the liver and digestive organs, and sorely test the doctor's judgment, whether brain or stomach be the cause of this effect defective:—

"For this effect, defective, comes from cause."

But Shakspere, when he wrote the play, was in the same state of mind as Hamlet; of course he had not a father murdered, a mother incestuously married, nor had he seen a ghost; yet still he was in a very similar predicament. He was suffering under the pangs of a rejected play; he saw himself surpassed by Marlowe as a tragic writer; he saw his just and reasonable ambition of becoming a distinguished dramatist passing from the regions of reality into the semblance of an airy nothingness; and he had quarrelled with two of his most intimate friends. Let us compare his position with Hamlet's :—

Hamlet.	*Shakspere.*
A father murdered and in purgatory.	A play damned, the author in purgatory.
A mother's incestuous marriage.	Dead beat by Marlowe.
Has to kill his uncle.	The chance of two duels on his hands.
Has seen a ghost.	Has seen the ghost of his own ambition.

No wonder Shakspere, like Hamlet, has bad dreams, and views the world with a jaundiced eye; and had this play been damned, and followed the fate of Dido and Æneas, Shakspere's own mind might have become unhinged, as Hamlet's is supposed to have been; there would have been no *Love's Labour's Lost*, or at least with the part of Biron omitted; for the soundest intellect must be influenced by external circumstances as well as by the state of its earthly tenement; if wonderfully, so are we fearfully made.

Let us now examine the ghost; no mortal has hitherto ever ventured to do so; perhaps religious awe forbids the summoning a spiritual being before a human tribunal; but is he really a spirit or only moonshine? in either case he declines answering the summons; so the only way to get at him is for his Majesty to have the Prince tried for the murder of Polonius. During the trial it is brought out, the ghost was seen on three successive nights, at the same hour and place, and in armour; that the Prince cross-questioned Horatio minutely about his being arm'd; and was afterwards overheard talking to himself, "my father's spirit in arms! all is not well; I doubt some foul play." That on the fourth night, the Prince, violently excited, followed the ghost a short distance alone, and to his friends, who soon afterwards joined him, he spoke "wild and hurling words;" his own statement of what the ghost had said, was adduced as corroborative evidence against him; for it was proved the ghost said nothing on the first three nights, nor had the officers heard anything on the fourth night, excepting a sound like "swear," which was proved to be the reverberation of a "fellow in the cellarage," calling out "where is it," meaning the coal-box. It was then ably argued by the counsel for the prosecution, that the ghost was a ghost-story, all moonshine as usual; what was the ghost then? simply, like the spectre of the Brocken, an image reflected from the King's statue, which had just been erected at the entrance to the Castle; that the waving of the arm was merely an undulation of the air; as the Prince advanced towards the figure, it receded by a well-known law in optics, and when he stopped and said, he would go no further, the figure politely stopped also. It was then clearly and succinctly pointed out, that the speech of the said ghost was merely the Prince's imagination, his own thoughts; for he is told literally nothing but what he knew before, and the rest was a wretched suspicion, based on a partial knowledge of the action of drugs; at this point the Prince was heard to mutter, " the unkindest cut of all ;" and the Court was startled by a deep groan, when the learned counsel amidst an audible applause, clenched the subject by observing, How can a ghost speak, when he has no bodily or material organs? It was further proved, that in the Queen's chamber the ghost was not visible to her, nor was it armed, as shown by the Prince's remark, "in his habit as he lived;" this was adduced as additional evidence, that the ghost on the platform was merely a reflection in the air; and it was further shown, that the said ghost's speech in the chamber, was only an echo or reflection of the Prince's own thoughts, of his own speech :—

> *Ham.* " Do you not come your tardy son to chide,
> That, laps'd in time and passion, lets go by
> The important acting of your dread command ?
> O, say.
>
> *Ghost.* Do not forget: This visitation
> Is but to whet thy almost blunted purpose ;"

and the following lines of the ghost were merely the

utterance of the Prince's own feelings on seeing his mother looking amazed at him.

The verdict was, guilty of the death of Polonius, with a recommendation to mercy as a monomaniac; and the Judge condemned him to transportation for life, to the penal settlements in England, where his spirit has ever since dwelt, not only mad himself, but the cause of a literary lunacy among many others. All concerned in the prosecution were handsomely rewarded, and remained ever afterwards firm supporters of the government; the learned Judge was for his valuable services promoted by his Majesty to be Lord Chancellor, and soon after stepped into the shoes of old Polonius.

We thus make the astounding discovery, that the Danish Prince is a monomaniac, whilst Hamlet is perfectly sane. The Prince, in consequence of the sudden death of his father, and his mother's hasty marriage, on hearing Horatio's account of his "father's spirit in arms," immediately suspects "all is not right;" and on seeing what was probably a mere reflection in the air, his heated imagination becomes excited to phrensy, and under this excitement, the impression remains on the retina, and he continues seeing the supposed ghost in his mind's eye; on the arrival of his friends, the wild and hurling words denote a mind already affected; with the cunning and half-consciousness of his condition, he tells them not to be surprised, should he "put an antick disposition on." It is thus evident, Shakspere knew what a ghost was; and it has already been shown, the words of the ghost in the Queen's chamber were merely the Prince's own thoughts; no wonder his mother exclaimed, "poor boy, alas, he's mad." But with regard to Hamlet, the case is altered; *his* ghost is a reality, which nobody can deny; unfortunately Shakspere has forgotten to tell us how to call spirits from the vasty deep and make them visible and audible; Hamlet therefore is perfectly sane. We may then sum up,—the Danish Prince is a monomaniac; but Hamlet himself is the healthy Shakspere, not "a lame limb of the law," but

> "An apothecary's apprentice,
> The student of nature."

Postscript.—On making a careful examination of the preceding analysis, we find the following important passage, the address of Hamlet to Laertes, has by some unaccountable oversight, been omitted:—

Ham. "Give me your pardon, sir; I have done you wrong;
But pardon 't, as you are a gentleman.
This presence knows, and you must needs have heard,
How I am punish'd with a sore distraction.
What I have done,
That might your nature, honour, and exception,
Roughly awake, I here proclaim was madness."—
Hamlet, act v., scene 2.

This passage has given great offence, under the supposition Hamlet is uttering a deliberate falsehood, "*a direct lie,*" since he said in the first act, he should feign madness, and actually did so, only an hour or two ago, on leaving the churchyard; and in the chamber-scene had solemnly assured his mother, he was only "mad in craft;" but, happily, this supposition of his falsehood is altogether a misapprehension.

The sea-voyage had effectually cleared Hamlet's biliary system; and he re-appears in this fifth act a wiser and a sadder man. When he justifies himself to Horatio, "is't not perfect conscience to quit him with this arm," he does so in a straightforward and rational manner, without hinting a word about the ghost and the dread command; and, when he slays Claudius, there is not any exhibition of the same fiend-like vindictiveness as in the third act. His estimate also of Laertes' conduct,

> "For by the image of my cause, I see
> The portraiture of his,"

differs widely from his treatment of Guildenstern and Rosencrantz; in the one case he manifests a clear and healthy judgment; but in his behaviour to his two school-fellows, the *precursory symptoms* of an attack of insanity are very apparent,—" distrustful of friends and relatives, very fretful and irascible on slight occasions; subject to a kind of uneasiness, which he cannot describe or account for," *Essay on Insanity*; and thus when Hamlet says to Laertes, "What I have done, I here proclaim was madness," he speaks the simple truth; for *he is now conscious*, that each appearance of the ghost was a temporary hallucination, produced by the violent excitement, under which at the moment he was labouring. —There is no moral obliquity of vision in Shakspere, "if then you do not like him, surely you are in some manifest danger, not to understand him."

As Hamlet in the first four acts is influenced or governed by one predominant idea, a false impression, an hallucination, he must consequently be insane, and his feigned madness a real madness. His insanity is that form of monomania,* which is combined with melancholia and depression, and the poet has with admirable skill and judgment shown the latter symptom following each paroxysm of maniacal excitement; *vide* Hamlet's speech at the end of the first act, and again in act fourth, scene fourth. Consequently the omissions in the folio are omissions of the players; this is very evident in Hamlet's speech in the queen's chamber, where the passages are omitted, the points of the daggers he would speak to his mother, being at the time in a state of maniacal excitement. The exclamation of Claudius, in act fourth, scene third, " alas, alas!" can only be a hypocritical expression of sympathy, and the omission of the passage is most probably a slip of the compositor.

---

* *Monomania*, or partial insanity, is that form of mental derangement in which there exists some prominent and fixed delusion, giving a tone to the whole character, feelings, and conduct of the individual. It was to this form of insanity that Locke's famous dictum especially applied, when he said of madmen, that "they reasoned correctly on false premises."

"The intellect, also, in the *melancholic* is usually clear and composed, unable only to resist the morbid depression or the hopeless delusions that spring from it and feed it." They are also very positive about their sanity, asserting the same with the utmost precision and calmness of manner; and though "an acuteness of wit belongs to most of the varieties," yet the discursive faculty of reason is often affected; as Hamlet says,—"Shall we to the court? for, by my fay, I cannot reason;"—but it is otherwise in the scene with Osric, in the fifth act, which is probably intended as a contrast or counter-scene to this very passage in act second, scene second; in the one, Hamlet is unable to carry on a chain of reasoning,—in the other, his mind is clear and collected, notwithstanding his being so ill at heart.—

Hor. "His purse is empty already; all his golden words are spent."
Ham. "Do but blow them to their trials, the bubbles are out."
Act v., scene 2.

It should also be noted as evidence of Shakspere's wonderful art, that the first appearance of the ghost is not purely *subjective*, but has an *objective* cause; and again in the queen's chamber the ghost is preceded by Hamlet's intense gaze at his father's picture, "in his habit as he lived." We need not then be surprised at his recovery under the kind and respectful attention of the pirates, who love and reverence him as their prince, together with the beneficial action of a sea-sickness, of the sea-air, and absolute rest from all excitement.

But the other parties on the platform do not labour under an hallucination; they saw a something, which in their frightened imaginations and according to the notions of those times they supposed to be a ghost; theirs was merely an error of judgment; and had the matter been explained to them, they would more or less readily, according to their faith in ghosts, have acknowledged the same.*

It is scarcely credible, considering his other engagements and studies, Shakspere could have applied himself so diligently and earnestly, and have acquired during his residence in London such a mastery over the theory and practice of physic as is exhibited in Hamlet, unless he had previously received some professional instruction.

---

* Although the ghost of Banquo is an hallucination, an image purely subjective, yet Macbeth is not mad like Hamlet; he quickly recovers himself and recognizes it as the phantasm of his own guilty soul:—"Hence, horrible shadow! Unreal mockery, hence!" As

According to Rowe, "it is without controversy, Shakspere had no knowledge of the writings of the ancient poets;" Pope also speaks of him, as being without that knowledge of the best models, the ancients, to inspire him *with an emulation of them;* and so it is echoed up to the present day. Dr. Johnson observes, "whether Shakspere knew the unities and rejected them by design, or deviated from them by happy ignorance, it is, I think, impossible to decide, and useless to inquire. We may reasonably suppose, that when he rose to notice, he did not want the counsels and admonitions of scholars and critics; and that he at last deliberately persisted in a practice, which he might have begun by chance." Perhaps it is not "so impossible to decide and useless to inquire," as the learned lexicographer supposes in this passage of lucky guesses; and although, like Shakspere, I have but small Latin and less Greek, still the story of Hamlet so strongly reminds one of the story of the House of Atreus, I thought it advisable to look into a translation of the Greek tragedies, and I find myself amply repaid for the trouble.

When Nash accused him of stealing from Seneca, Shakspere must have chuckled and curled his lip with disdain, knowing he had been poaching in a far more aristocratic preserve; that he had been conning over the Orestes and the masterpieces of the Greek drama; he found them apparently "a little more than kin and less than

---

Hamlet is undeniably a monomaniac, all the learned disquisitions upon him must henceforth be regarded as a poetical delusion; and his critics have the delightful task of commencing a new series, sane essays on an insane subject, the national drama of England.

kind," for he bagged but very little game; though unmistakably Pylades lives again in Horatio.

Considering the circumstances and the situation of the two parties, there is a strong analogy and resemblance between Horatio's speech at the end of the first scene, and the following extract from the commencement of the *Electra of Sophocles* :—

> *Tutor.* "Now therefore, O Orestes, and you, O Pylades, dearest of friends, we must quickly deliberate what we ought to do. Since already the bright beam of the sun is making audible to us the morning song of the birds; and the dark night of stars has departed. Before then any man comes forth from his house deliberate in counsel, since we are in a situation where it is no longer time to hesitate, but the crisis requires action."

> *Hor.* " So have I heard, and do in part believe it;
> But see the sun in russet mantle clad,
> Walks o'er the dew of yon high mountain top,
> Break we our watch up, and by my advice,
> Let us impart what we have seen to-night
> Unto young Hamlet; for upon my life
> This Spirit dumb to us will speak to him:
> Do you consent, we shall acquaint him with it,
> As needful in our love, fitting our duty?"
>
> Ed. 1603.

It appears to me, that it is to this line, " the bright beam of the sun is making audible to us the morning song of the birds," we owe the beautiful passage, "The cock that is the trumpet to the morn," as well as "the sun in russet mantle clad;" and in the amended copy the poet has judiciously altered *sun* into *morn*.

In the commencement of the *Iphigenia in Aulis*, which is also a night scene, the following lines remind us of Bernardo's statement :—

Agam.   "What star is that
             There sailing?
Att.   Sirius in his middle height
             Near the sev'n Pleiads riding.
Agam.   Not the sound
             Of birds is heard, nor of the sea; the winds
             Are hush'd in silence on the Euripus."
                                    Iphigenia in Aulis.

Ber. "Have you had quiet guard?
Fran.   Not a mouse stirring.
Hor.   Well sit we down,
        And let us hear Bernardo speak of this.
Ber. Last night of all,
        When yon same star, that's westward from the pole,
        Had made his course to illume that part of heaven
        Where now it burns, Marcellus, and myself,
        The bell then beating one———"—
                                    Hamlet, act i., scene 1.

However slight the resemblance and coincidence of these passages may appear to the reader, yet there cannot be the least doubt the second scene in *Hamlet* is a paraphrase of the "second scene" in the *Electra of Sophocles,* between Electra and Chorus, as may be judged by the following extracts; Hamlet's expression "like Niobe,* all tears," is confirmation strong; Hamlet soliloquizes, so does Electra:—

Cho. "O Electra, child of a most wretched mother, how unceasingly you are thus ever uttering lamentations for Agamemnon.
Elec. But I do not wish to abandon this habit, so as not to mourn for my miserable father.
Cho. But not at all either by lamentations or prayers will you raise your father from the all-receiving gulf of Pluto; but proceeding from moderate to unreasonable grief, continually

---

* "Shakspere caught this idea from an ancient ballad."—*Steevens.*

lamenting, you destroy yourself. Why do you love grief, as I see you do, in which there is no relief from misfortune?

Elec. O miserable Niobe, but I consider you a goddess, thou who in your tomb of stone ever weepest.

Cho. Grief has not appeared to you alone of mortals, O my child, in lamenting which you exceed those who are within, from the same source with whom you are sprung and are akin to them in family.

Cho. Beware of saying more. It is not right to quarrel with the powerful so as to provoke them;—Death is the natural fate of all mortals."

and further on Electra says, that her mother thus abuses her:—

"O thou impious object of hatred, have you alone lost a father, and is no other mortal in affliction."

and towards the end of the play Electra thus speaks to the Tutor:—

"Hail, O father, for I think I see my father, hail, and know that of all men I have most hated and most loved you in one day."

The following extracts remind us of Hamlet's address to his mother in her bed-chamber:—

Elec. "And when I see the crowning insult of all, the murderer in my father's bed with my wretched mother, if I may call her a mother who sleeps with him, but she is so shameless that she cohabits with the polluter, fearing no fury, but as it were triumphing in her deeds. Such speeches she howls out, and being present at the same time, her illustrious bridegroom excites her to the same course, that thorough coward, that entire evil, he who fights his battles with the aid of women.

The following passages remind us of the ghost:—

"Like to the god perchance some demon spoke."

Electra of Euripides.

"Had these eyes seen my father, had I ask'd him
In duty if I ought to slay my mother,

> I think he would have pray'd me not to plunge
> My murdering sword in her that gave me birth."
>
> "Yet my soul
> Was struck with horror, 'lest some vengeful power
> Spake this, which I misdeem'd thy voice divine."—
>
> *Orestes.*

The first line may have been merely a coincidence, but the observation of Orestes, that his father would have prayed him not to kill his mother, strongly impresses on us the opinion, Shakspere must have read these two tragedies:—

Ghost. "But howsoever, let not thy heart
Conspire against thy mother aught,
Leave her to heaven,
And to the burthen that her conscience bears."

Ham. "My mother she has sent to speak with me;
O God, let ne'er the heart of Nero enter
This soft bosom.
Let me be cruel, not unnatural.
I will speak daggers, those sharp words being spent,
To do her wrong my soul shall ne'er consent."—
Ed. 1603.

As Orestes praises his friend, so does Hamlet; the parallel passages are too similar to be accidental:—

Orest. "Life hath no blessing like a prudent friend;"

"But I forbear
Nor with intemperate praise thine ear offend."

Ham. "Horatio, thou art e'en as just a man,"—
"Nay why should I flatter thee?"—Ed. 1603.

Pylad. "Should'st thou but hope I would survive thy death."

Orest. "O save thee for thy father, die not with me,
Thou hast a country.

Pylad. Together will I die with thee and her."—

Orestes.

> *Hor.* No, I am more an antike Roman,
>   Then a Dane, here is some poison left.
> *Ham.* Upon my love I charge thee let it go."—Ed. 1603.

The scene also, where Hamlet questions Horatio about the appearance of the ghost, is probably an imitation of the dialogue between Ædipus and Iocasta about the murder of Laius in *Ædipus Tyrannus*.

These extracts irresistibly prove, that Shakspere, before composing Hamlet, must have devoted much time and thought to the study of the Greek drama. He was certainly no profound Greek scholar, and aimed not at being "an old-clothes philosopher;" yet he looked, as no man else ever did, into the very souls of the Greek dramatists, face to face. That he read not only *Sophocles* and *Euripides*, but *Æschylus* also, is beyond a doubt; for who is Ophelia, the virgin sacrificed to Diana? who is she, but the Iphigenia of Æschylus, the meek, submissive, sacrificial lamb; surely we may say, and not irreverently, such a wonderful re-creation is more nearly allied to the spirit of God than to the genius of man:—

> "Arm'd in a woman's cause, around
>   Fierce for the war the princes rose;
> No place affrighted pity found.
> In vain the virgin's streaming tear,
> Her cries in vain, her pleading pray'r,
>   Her agonizing woes.
> Could the fond father hear unmov'd?
> The Fates decreed; the king approv'd;
> Then to th' attendants gave command
> Decent her flowing robes to bind;

    Prone on the altar with strong hand
        To place her, like a spotless hind;
    And check her sweet voice, that no sound
    Unhallow'd might the rites confound.
Rent on the earth her maiden veil she throws
        That emulates the rose;
    And on the sad attendants rolling
The trembling lustre of her dewy eyes,
      Their grief-impassion'd souls controlling,
    That ennobled, modest grace,
    Which the mimic pencil tries
    In the imag'd form to trace,
        The breathing picture shows;
    And as, amidst his festal pleasures,
          Her father oft rejoic'd to hear
    Her voice in soft mellifluous measures
        Warble the sprightly fancied air;
So now in act to speak the virgin stands:
    But when, the third libation paid,
        She heard her father's dread commands
    Injoining silence, *she obey'd;*
        And for her country's good,
With *patient meek submissive mind*
        To her hard fate resigned,
Pour'd out the rich stream of her blood."—
                      The Agamemnon.

Mrs. Jameson says of Ophelia, "in her the feminine character appears resolved into its very elementary principles—*modesty, grace,* and tenderness;" and did she not for two long months "with patient, meek, submissive mind" "repel his letters and deny his access to her," as she promised her father, "I shall obey, my lord."

But the tender and most tragic Euripides could not conceive such a character; he makes a wretched mess of the affair by portraying Iphigenia as going, like an Electra, triumphantly to the sacrifice, and then saves her life at the altar. Aristotle knew better, old Æschylus knew better, so did Shakspere, and so did Miss Bronte; her prim, starch, but plucky little governess, notwithstanding the entreaties of her kind old father, is sacrificed to the goddess Diana, her heart perishes with Monsieur Paul in the storm.

But Goethe's *Iphigenia*, however beautiful as a dramatic poem, is not a re-creation; it is merely a modern copy of the *Iphigenia of Euripides*, or rather a christianised Electra; for the foundation of each character is based on a deep religious sense of duty. And Goethe's opinion about Hamlet's weakness, "a great action laid upon a soul unfit for the performance of it," is far more applicable to Orestes,* nor is it inapplicable to Agamemnon himself; the following lines correspond remarkably with the passage quoted by Goethe:—

Agam.   "O that this high honour
         Some other had received not I."
    "Distraction's in the thought, unhappy me.
      My misery sinks me."

                              Iphigenia in Aulis.

---

* Orestes in *Æschylus*, is undeniably mad; but in *Euripides* his madness is at least problematical. He appears to have had an attack of remittent fever, and in the course of six days wasted away to a mere skeleton; and afterwards he became subject to epileptic fits:—
    Herdsman.   "But his frenzy of its force
         Abating, on the earth the stranger falls,
         Foam bursting from his mouth."—
                              Iphigenia in Tauris.

Possibly Euripides may also have been an apothecary's apprentice, or at least a student in medicine; Socrates, his intimate friend, is said to have been an accoucheur, though some pretend, he only practised in cerebral midwifery, infants of the brain.

Ham. "The time is out of joint; O cursed spite!
That ever I was born to set it right."—Ed. 1603.
Ores. "Like to the god perchance some demon spoke.
Elec. What, from the sacred tripod! vain surmise.
Ores. Ne'er can my reason deem this answer just.
Elec. Sink not unmann'd, to weak and timorous thoughts."
Electra of Euripides.

It is astonishing with what amazing self-confidence and originality this Warwickshire lad measures himself with the mightiest names of Greece, names at that time held by all other men as gods, as something divine and superhuman; whatever he touches he turns to gold, or purifies it through the fire of his own genius; who but a Shakspere could have translated the madness of Orestes into the monomaniac and simulated madness of Hamlet? and who, but a poetical doctor, could have metempsychosed Apollo into a ghost? "the god of poesie and physicke;" and such a ghost! never in the most high and palmy state of Greece did Apollo appear to mortal eyes so like a god, so like a spirit of the other world.

Porson, in some remarks on the three great tragedians of Greece, observes, that the language of Euripides "pleases us by its natural simplicity and plainness,— though sometimes it descends too much towards the humble and ordinary style." "Sophocles, on the contrary, while he is anxious to avoid vulgar phraseology, and plebeian modes of expression, is somewhat too prone to indulge in forced metaphors, harsh inversions of language, and other faults of that nature, which render his verses, at times, too obscure to be pleasing."—*Porson's Life by Watson,* p. 108.

This passage is just as applicable to the later dramas

of Shakspere as to the tragedies of Sophocles; and as Shakspere is said to have a greater affinity in his genius to Sophocles, than to either of the other Greek dramatists, the question arises, is this similarity of style an accidental resemblance, or an imitation?

As we occasionally meet with critical remarks, such as, "there is something very Greekish in this,"—"we have here another instance of Shakspere's profound knowledge of poetic story,"—"the Greek dramatists,* whose practice Shakspere follows in many things, whether knowingly or unconsciously,"—and as Macbeth is said to have some analogy to the Electra of Sophocles and to the Trilogy of Æschylus, it follows as the more reasonable explanation, that Shakspere must have had a far more intimate knowledge of the Greek language, than the warmest supporters of his classical learning have given him credit for.

Mr. Armitage Brown jumped to the conclusion, that *Hamlet* was written before the autumn of 1589, and is supported therein by Mr. Knight; but there are plausible grounds for this opinion, not noticed by these gentlemen; Shakspere must have been forcibly struck by the extraordinary success of *Tamburlaine* and *Faustus*; and it seems as if the latter play gave rise to *Hamlet*; for who and what is he? Shakspere, meditating a new tragedy, and looking out for a suitable subject, fortunately looked in, and found what he wanted, a philosopher and a wit, Faustus and Mephistophiles in one. Happily his philosophy and wit are always on the side of religion and morality; though these tendencies are

---

* Hartley Coleridge, in a note to *Massinger*, p. xxxviii.

not so distinctly visible in the witty philosopher of France, nor in the author of the German *Faust*.

We may then easily imagine, how *Hamlet* arose in the poet's mind;—he selects the story from *Saxo Grammaticus* as the sketch or outline of the play; perceives its resemblance to the old Greek story of Orestes, but unluckily he has no god at his command, the doctors having rejected Apollo, and retained, as usual with mankind, the worst part only, the snake as their emblem; he meditates over his difficulties, "Ah there's the rub! about my brains! ha! ha! the ghost's the thing." So he pours into the witches' cauldron nine Greek tragedies, tumbles Faustus and Mephistophiles on the top of them, and then, like Curtius for his country's good, plunges over head and ears into the cauldron himself, and reappears as—Hamlet the Dane.

But he borrows not nature from these classical divinities; he returns to nature and himself, to Pericles; for is not Pericles Hamlet? at least, "a piece of him":—

> "If thou livest, Pericles, thou hast a heart
> That even cracks for woe."

As both Potter and Francklin, in their translations, adopt the very phrases used in *Hamlet*, it is curious if they never suspected Shakspere may have read these tragedies; it shows very clearly, how injurious, how benumbing to the mind, are prejudices and preconceived opinions.

It may be reasonably inferred from the words of Marcellus:—

> "And why such daily cast of brazen cannon,
> And foreign mart for implements of war:
> Why such impress of shipwrights,"

that *Hamlet* was composed during the summer of 1588, and was brought out in the winter season some weeks before Christmas. I have previously shown that Shakspere must have gone to London in 1585, taking up to town with him Pericles, a modest, amiable young man; the success of this play encouraged him, gave him more swing and confidence, so that he speaks out more freely and boldly, and manifests himself more openly in *Valentine*. We may then suppose he brought out *Pericles* in 1585, *Valentine* in the spring of 1586, and *Titus Andronicus* the following Christmas; and in the spring of 1587, as I shall hereafter show, *All's Well that Ends Well*. About the same period Marlowe produced *Tamburlaine*, say, both parts in 1586; *Faustus* is considered to have appeared in 1588, and probably as early as December, '87; Shakspere, constantly studying the principles of his art, and struck with the great popularity of *Tamburlaine*, brings forth, not as a vulgar imitator, but as a young artist, *Dido* and *Æneas* at Christmas, 1587. We may imagine what must have been his feelings; how galled and wounded, how disgusted with himself and with the world! He, conscious of his own superiority as a poet, finds himself a successful comic writer, but has failed in his highest ambition, in tragedy; whilst Marlowe has written three tragedies, each a popular favourite, and the last far superior to the two parts of *Tamburlaine*. There can be little doubt Marlowe at this moment was in the public opinion [though certainly not by the judicious few] regarded as the greater genius of the two.

Hamlet, however, was more than successful; it created a tremendous sensation, and took London by storm. Then Shakspere, flushed with his triumph, poured forth the rejoicings of his soul in *Love's Labour's Lost;* no longer did "this brave o'er-hanging—this majestical roof fretted with golden fire, appear no other thing to him than a foul and pestilent congregation of vapours;" all nature laughed around him; he had vanquished his enemies, and, hurling the giants down, he seated himself on the dramatic throne, as on a rock environed by the sea, smiling at the multitudinous waves of barbarism roaring around him; and Biron was the expression of his exultant feelings.

Hamlet and Biron must, then, be regarded as the same person; "the clouds hang on" the one, and the other is "too much i' the sun;" "the gibing spirit" is strong in Hamlet, and had the joyous-hearted and chivalrous Biron seen the ghost of a murdered father, and his mother been guilty of an incestuous marriage, he too, "the wit, poet, and philosopher," would have been as melancholy, contemplative, and decisive, as Hamlet; like him, he soliloquizes, and is the main character, the master-spirit in the play; it is the same man under different circumstances:—

> "The courtier's, scholar's, soldier's eye, tongue, sword:
> The expectancy and rose of the fair state,
> The glass of fashion, and the mould of form,
> The observ'd of all observers!"

Is not *that* the character of Biron, and was it not the

character of Hamlet previous to his father's death? Had Goethe known the connecting link between these two plays, he would have saved himself the trouble of speculating about Hamlet's natural character. There cannot be the slightest doubt, the lecture of Rosaline is an honest confession of one of Shakspere's own failings, too fond of jesting, a fault which he felt quite unqualified him for success in the medical trade, and so, like a sensible man, he cut it, that is, the trade.

In the supplementary notice to the *Two Gentlemen of Verona, Pictorial Shakspere*, we read: "In the first scene he (Valentine) laughs at the passion of Proteus, as if he knew that it was alien to his nature; but when he has become enamoured himself, with what enthusiasm he proclaims his devotion:—

" Why man she is mine own;
And I as rich in having such a jewel
As twenty seas, if all their sand were pearl."

"In this passionate admiration we have the germ of Romeo, and so also in the scene where Valentine is banished:—

' And why not death, rather than living torment.'

"We are not wandering from our purpose of contrasting Proteus and Valentine, by showing that the character of Valentine is compounded of some of the elements that we find in Romeo."

But Biron is also a similar character, compounded of the same elements; with what enthusiasm he proclaims his devotion:—

" Who sees the heavenly Rosaline,
That, like a rude and savage man of Inde,

> At the first opening of the gorgeous east,
> Bows not his vassal head; and, strucken blind,
> Kisses the base ground with obedient breast?"

They are three brothers, or rather three manifestations of the same spirit re-appearing at different periods, and under different circumstances. Coleridge thus speaks of Biron's celebrated speech:—"It is logic clothed in rhetoric;—but observe how Shakspere, in his two-fold being of poet and philosopher, avails himself of it to convey profound truths in the most lively images,—the whole remaining *faithful to the character supposed* to utter the lines, and the expressions themselves constituting a further development of that character."

But Biron is not "the germ," "the pre-existent state" of Benedick, the type of all that is elegant and fascinating; nor Rosaline of Beatrice; Biron is a far higher and loftier character; Benedick may be, as Horatio would say, "a piece of him;" *he* was played upon; but had any one attempted to play upon Biron, they would have caught a Tartar; no one ever succeeded in that game, save and except *one man*.

In the wit-combats at the *Mermaid* between Shakspere and Jonson, Ben had very little chance with his opponent, who was "an old sworder" at the game, and had in his younger days played at the cudgels with a far more formidable competitor. I allude to the wit-combats between Shakspere and Lyly at the *Mitre*, where the gentle Willy met his match; the combatants were thoroughly good-humoured, for each could take as well as give. Nobody rejoiced more in the success of *Hamlet* than John Lyly; and he had shown his love and esteem for Shakspere on a former occasion in a most marked and flattering manner.

In the comedy of *Endymion*, Cynthia is supposed to represent Queen Elizabeth, and no doubt her gracious majesty appropriated to herself all the compliments, as the courtly poet intended. But under this superficial allegory was concealed a far more beautiful and poetical one. Endymion is the youthful poet, in love with Tellus, or nature, but loving, worshipping in a far higher degree Cynthia, the poetry of nature; for of poetry, as of the moon or Cynthia, it may be said, the form is ever changing, but the spirit is the same. Is then Endymion himself merely a poetical conception, a poet's dream, or a living reality? His friend Eumenides is unmistakably John Lyly, the satirical wit:—

Cynth. "Endymion you must now tell who Eumenides shrineth for his saint.
End. Semele, Madame.
Cynth. Semele, Eumenides? is it Semele? the very wasp of all women, whose tongue stingeth as much as an adder's tooth?
Eum. It is Semele, Cynthia; the possession of whose love must only prolong my life."—Act v., scene 3.

That Shakspere is Endymion may be deduced from the following circumstances:—In the opening of the comedy, Endymion says, "my thoughts, Eumenides, are stitched to the stars, which being as high as I can see, thou maist imagine, how much higher they are than I can reach." This passage is an allusion to the line in the *Two Gentlemen of Verona* :—

"Wilt thou reach stars, because they shine on thee;"
which line again was in fact a complimentary quotation from Campaspe, where Apelles says, "stars are to be looked, not reach'd at."

Again in *Endymion* :—

Epi. "Why, you know it is said, the tide tarrieth no man.
Sam. True.
Epi. A monstrous lie, for I was tied two hours, and tarried for one to unlose me."

The expression, "you know it is said," is evidently an acknowledgment, a direct complimentary reference to a well-known and humourous scene in a popular comedy :—

Pan. "Away, ass; you will lose the tide, if you tarry any longer.
Launce. It is no matter if the tied were lost; for it is the unkindest tied, that ever man tied.
Pan. What's the unkindest tide?
Launce. Why, he that's tied here, Crab, my dog."—
Two Gentlemen of Verona, act ii., scene 3.

These two allusions, the stars and the pun, clearly point at Shakspere as being the youthful poet Endymion; but since it is generally supposed Shakspere borrowed the pun as well as the stars, let us examine into the dates of these three plays; *Campaspe* was published in 1584, the *Two Gentlemen of Verona* was most probably written in 1586, and *Endymion* in 1587; for in act third, scene fourth, Eumenides soliloquizes, "how secret hast thou been these seven years?" now *Euphues* was published in 1580; and again, Endymion says, "remembering my solitary life almost these seven years, whom have I entertained but mine own thoughts and thy virtues?" Shakspere at this time was in his twenty-fourth year, so that his consciousness of poetical inspiration as being a votary of the Muses dates from his seventeenth year, not an unreasonable supposition.

Having thus from internal evidence established the date of the play, and that Endymion and Eumenides are Shakspere and Lyly, we can readily understand the whole drift of the allegory; at the instigation of Tellus, Endymion is thrown into a deep sleep by the enchantress Dipsas, and is re-awakened by a kiss from Cynthia; or in other words, Shakspere, having written two plays full of poetry and nature, falls asleep under the hands of the goddess of dulness, or bad taste, and writes *Titus Andronicus*, a tale of horrors; his poetical genius soon after pricks his conscience, he awakens and perceives the error he has committed.

Side by side, and parallel with Endymion, runs the character of Sir Tophas, the bragging soldier, with Epi his page, a most ridiculous and amusing caricature of Marlowe; the dulness of the wit is intentional on the author's part and in character:—

Epi. "Nothing hath made my master a fool but flat scholarship."

"*O lepidum caput*, O madcap master! you were worthy to win Dipsas, were she as old again, for in your love you have worn the nap of your wit quite off and made it threadbare."—Act v., scene 2.

Top. "Why fool, a poet is as much as one should say, a poet. But soft, yonder be two wrens, shall I shoot at them?

Epi. They are two lads.

Top. Larks or wrens, I will kill them.
Epi. Larks? are you blind? they are two little boys.
Dar. Why, Sir Tophas, have you forgotten your old friends?
Act i., scene 3.

These two larks or wrens are of course the two parts of *Tamburlaine,* otherwise the whole passage is merely silly, childish nonsense; to add to the humour, the two little boys are pages to Endymion and Eumenides. Like Endymion, Sir Tophas falls in love, but with Dipsas, and has an absurd dream of an owl [with the face of Dipsas] the bird of wisdom, for Marlowe was a learned man:—

Top. "Learned? I am all Mars and Ars.
Sam. Nay, you are all mass and ass.
Top. Mock you me? you shall both suffer, yet with such weapons, as you shall make choice of the weapon, wherewith you shall perish. Am I all a mass or lump, is there no proportion in me? am I all ass? is there no wit in me? Epi, prepare them to the slaughter.
Sam. I pray, sir, hear us speak? we call you mass, which your learning doth well understand is all man, for Mas maris is a man. Then As [as you know] is a weight, and we for your virtues account you a weight.
Top. The Latin hath saved your lives."—Act i., scene 3.

The following passage is evidently a caricature of Tamburlaine's love for Zenocrate;—on hearing of Dipsas being married, Sir Tophas meditates suicide:—

Top. "O heavens, an husband? What death is agreeable to my fortune?
Sam. Be not desperate, and we will help you to find a young lady.
Top. I love no grissels they are so brittle, they will crack like glass, or so dainty, that if they be touched, they are

straight of the fashion of wax; *animus majoribus instat.* I desire old matrons. What a sight would it be to embrace one whose hair were as orient as the pearl! whose teeth shall be so pure a watchet, that they shall stain the truest turkis! whose nose shall throw more beams from it than the fiery carbuncle! whose eyes shall be environed about with redness exceeding the deepest coral! And whose lips might compare with silver for the paleness! Such a one if you can help me to, I will by piece-meal curtal my affections towards *Dipsas*, and walk my swelling thoughts 'till they be cold."

Tamb. "Zenocrate, lovelier than the love of Jove,
Brighter than is the silver Rhodope,
Fairer than whitest snow on Scythian hills."
"Zenocrate the loveliest maid alive,
Fairer than rocks of pearl and precious stone,
The only paragon of Tamburlaine.
Whose eyes are brighter than the lamps of heaven,
And speech more pleasant than sweet harmony;
That with thy looks can'st clear the darken'd sky,
And calm the rage of thundering Jupiter."

Sir Tophas must also, like Endymion, fall into a deep sleep.

But Endymion is very differently handled from Sir Tophas; in the concluding, as well as in the earlier scenes, the reality vividly and distinctly pierces through the allegorical covering; in describing his dream to Cynthia, Endymion says, "After long debating with herself, mercy overcame anger; and there appeared in her heavenly face such a divine majesty, mingled with a sweet mildness, that I was ravished with the sight above measure, and wished that I might have enjoyed the sight without end; and so she (Tellus) departed with the other ladies, of which the one (Dipsas) retained still an unmoveable cruelty, the other (Floscula) a constant pity;" and Cynthia, further on, observes:—

> "Endymion, continue as thou hast begun, and thou shalt find, that Cynthia shineth not on thee in vain.
> *End.* Your Highness hath blessed me, and your words have again restored my youth: methinks I feel my joints strong, and these mouldy hairs to molt, and all by your virtue, Cynthia, into whose hands the balance that weigheth time and fortune are committed.
> *Cynth.* What, young again? then it is pity to punish Tellus.
> *Tellus.* Ah, Endymion; now I know thee and ask pardon of thee; suffer me still to wish thee well."

Corsites, "a thirsty soul," who is appointed guardian of Tellus, is probably intended for Greene, who of all the giants was, perhaps, the least removed from nature. "No more than five dramas, the undoubted works of Greene have come down to posterity." He himself says in 1588, that he still maintains his "old course to palter up something in prose;" and it is to this double qualification, prose and poetry, that the following observations apply:—

> *Cor.* "Shall she work stories or poetries?
> *Cynth.* Could you not stir Endymion with that doubled strength of yours?"

Tellus says, "I marvel Corsites giveth me so much liberty; all the world knowing his charge to be so high, and his nature to be most strange; who hath so ill-intreated ladies of great honour, that he hath not suffered them to look out of windows, much less to walk abroad; it may be, he is in love with me."

It appears Greene treated the ladies rather ungallantly

in his plays and novels; and Nash in his *Anatomie of Absurditie*, 1589, ends one of his paragraphs thus:—
" Therefore, see how far they swerve from their purpose, who with *Greene* colours seek to garnish such Gorgon-like shapes."

Chettle says of Greene, "His hair was somewhat long;" and Harvey speaks of "his fond disguising of a Master of Art with ruffianly hair;" and Nash informs us, that "a jolly long red peake, like the spire of a steeple, he (Greene) cherisht continually without cutting, whereat a man might hang a jewel, it was so sharp and pendant."

We may now understand the following allusion :—

>*Cynth.* "But whom have we here,—is it not Corsites?
>*Zon.* It is; but more like a leopard than a man.
>*Cynth.* Awake him. How now, Corsites,—what make you here? How came you deformed? Look on thy hands, and then thou seest the picture of thy face."

Greene, in the epistle prefixed to *Perimedes*, 1588, says, he had been "had in derision by two gentlemen poets, &c.; I but answer in print what they have offered on the stage."

The two allusions in this comedy about the stars and the pun, should induce us to make a closer inspection of the *Two Gentlemen of Verona*; and then the supposition arises, that Panthino may be Lyly; for he is a scholar and a punster, probably his lordship's secretary, but certainly not a mere servant.

From the examination of these two comedies, *Endymion* and the *Two Gentlemen of Verona*, it may be surmised, these two *playwrights* were intimate friends, and that Lyly felt flattered by the compliment Shakspere paid him in quoting the line from *Campaspe,* and applying it so beautifully and so appropriately. On reviewing *Endymion* it strikes us also as something extraordinary, that Lyly should have advanced so far beyond the idea of all his contemporaries in analysing so accurately and poetically in 1587, the genius of Shakspere; this, perhaps, can only be accounted for on the supposition, that Shakspere in frequent conversations had laid open his heart to the inspection of his elder friend, freely exposing to him his innermost thoughts and aspirations;—no wonder Lyly was ravished with the sight, and worshipped that beautiful soul, that Psyche, the Warwickshire butterfly; a soul so different from Marlowe's, the book-worm, the moth.

On looking into *Pericles* we find this conjecture corroborated in a singular manner; for the whole play may be justly regarded as a hymn of praise to the goddess Diana or Cynthia, with an allusion to Tellus,—"*Marina.* No, no! I will rob Tellus of her weeds, to strew the green with *flowers;*" so that it contains the principal points of the allegory itself; and it is worthy of remark, this is the only allusion to Tellus in the whole Shaksperian drama, except in *Hamlet,* ed. 1604, "Tellus orbed ground."

In 1587, the same year in which *Endymion* was written, Nash in his epistles prefixed to Greene's *Menaphon,* thus writes :—" Idiot art-masters, that intrude themselves to our ears as the alchymists of eloquence, who (mounted on the stage of arrogance) think to outbrave better pens with the swelling bombast of bragging blank-verse." Hence it has been inferred, Greene must have been jealous of the success of *Tamburlaine;* but Lyly could not have been so affected; and the dry old humourist was just the man, like a bright particular star, to see through such a comet; and the exceedingly severe, the open and unconcealed ridicule of Marlowe as Sir Tophas, leads to the suspicion, there must have been a quarrel between them. This suspicion rises into certainty on examining *All's Well that Ends Well,* which must have been written about this time; not only is it acknowledged to be one of Shakspere's earlier plays, but the opening so strongly reminds us of *Hamlet,* that it may reasonably be conjectured to have been written in the preceding year. The remarks of the Countess to Helena and to Bertram, remind us of the king's words to Hamlet, and of Polonius' advice to his son; Helena's reply and soliloquy are in spirit identical with Hamlet's; there is in both scenes the same misapprehension, which is cleared up to the audience by the soliloquy; Helena weeps not for her father's death, but for Bertram's departure; and Hamlet's melancholy is caused, not by his father's death, but by his beloved mother's sinful marriage, that such an angel should have fallen:—

Hel. "O, were that all!—I think not on my father;
And these great tears grace his remembrance more
Than those I shed for him. What was he like?
I have forgot him: my imagination
Carries no favour in it, but Bertrams."

In this comedy there cannot be a doubt Parolles is a Shaksperian portrait of Marlowe:—

> *Hel.* "I know him a notorious liar,
> Think him a great way fool, solely a coward.
> *Hel.* Monsieur Parolles, you were born under a charitable star.
> *Par.* Under Mars, I."

He is also learned, "he hath a smack of all neighbouring languages;" like Sir Tophas, he is "all Mars and Ars;" Mr. Knight observes, "Parolles, from several passages, appears to have been intended for a great coxcomb in dress; to the insults of Lafeu the boaster has nothing to oppose,—neither wit nor courage." How well does all this coincide with what is really known of Marlowe. Nash calls him idiot art-master, full of arrogance; the Reverend Mr. Dyce represents him as irreligious, intemperate, with not even a moderate talent for the humourous:—

> "Now strutting in a silken sute,
> Then begging by the way."

Lord Lafeu must be regarded as a portrait of Lyly; besides genuine goodness of heart, he has also the caustic humour of Semele's lover; this opinion is strengthened by the expression, "he (Parolles) was first smoked by the old Lord Lafeu."

Let us now return to Lyly; besides *Endymion* he wrote three other comedies, evidently allegorical, *Sapho* and *Phao*, and *Campaspe*, both published in 1584, and *Gallathea* in 1592.

In *Sapho* and *Phao* the courtly poet has depicted the loves of Queen Elizabeth and the Duke of Anjou; the great difficulty with respect to this comedy is to decide, whether Hume copied Lyly, or Lyly, Hume; the only difference being, the one writes dramatically, the other historically. Hume says, "These reflections kept the Queen in great anxiety and irresolution; and she was observed to pass several nights without any sleep or repose. Soon after, he went over to his government of the Netherlands; lost the confidence of the states by a rash and violent attempt on their liberties; was expelled that country; retired into France, and there died:—

> *Sybilla.* "Do so, Phao; for destiny calleth thee as well from Sicily as from love. Other things hang over thy head, which I must neither tell, nor thou enquire. And so farewell."

The French Prince visited England in 1581, and died the same year as the comedy was published in 1584. In this comedy, *Pandion* has about him evident marks of the author, John Lyly; and the name reminds us of Panthino in the *Two Gentlemen of Verona*, originally spelt *Panthion*; like Semele in *Endymion*, his lady-love is rather waspish; he comes from Athens to Syracuse, as Lyly to London from Oxford.

In the comedy of *Campaspe* Queen Elizabeth might view her own virtues reflected in the chastity and warlike courage of Alexander. The loves of Apelles and Campaspe are probably an allusion to the marriage of the Earl of Leicester with the Countess of Essex.

In *Gallathea,* a virgin is sacrificed every five years to appease the wrath of Neptune; but at last the god, out of respect for Diana, (Queen Elizabeth), relents, and frees the land from the sea-monster, the Agar, by dispersing the Invincible Armada. The two pretty girls, Gallathea and Phillida, dressed as boys to escape being sacrificed, represent England and Scotland armed to resist the Spanish invasion; and their falling in love with one another and wishing to be married, must be an allusion to the probable union of the two countries under King James. This explanation of the allegory is strenghtened by the reference, twice repeated, to the *annus mirabilis,* '88. Thus it may be presumed, the comedy in its present form was produced about Christmas, 1588.

Let us now proceed and examine *Love's Labour's Lost,* in which Shakspere is supposed to satirize Euphuism in the character of Don Armado; and to have had particular individuals in view in the characters of *Holofernes* and *Boyet.* The curate, Sir Nathaniel, is probably intended for Lyly; the noting down in his tables, " a most singular and choice epithet," may have been a habit of Lyly's, for his comedies read like compositions, as if much of the wit had been collected and jotted down at intervals; they have not generally the easy flow and lightsome play of Shakspere's comedy.

" For this production, *Love's Labour's Lost,* Shakspere, it is presumed, found neither characters nor plot in any previous romance or drama;" but as he must have been as well acquainted with the comedy of *Endymion* as with *Euphues*, we may suspect Sir Tophas and Epi are the buds, which blossomed under the enchanter's wand into "the refined traveller of Spain" and that inimitable monkey, Moth; and the love of Don Armado for Jaquenetta, reminding us of the marriage of Sir Tophas with Dipsas' servant-maid Bagoa, raises the suspicion he is another variation, a flattering likeness of that unfortunate wight, Marlowe; who, if not, like Falstaff, witty himself, is at least the cause of much wit and humour in those two wags, our pleasant Willy and the Oxford Fiddlestick :

Scint. "You will be a good one if you live; but what is yonder formal fellow?
Dar. Sir Tophas, Sir Tophas, of whom we told you; if you be good wenches, make as though you love him, and wonder at him.
Favil. We will do our parts.
Dar. But first let us stand aside, and let him use his garb, for all consisteth in his gracing.
Favil. This passeth!
Scint. Why, is he not mad?
Sam. No, but a little vain-glorious."

Endymion, act ii., scene 2.

How closely does this agree with the description of Armado by Costard :—

"Armado o' the one side,—O, a most dainty man!
To see him walk before a lady, and to bear her fan;
To see him kiss his hand! and how most sweetly a'will swear!"

The King calls him "a man of complements," a formalist; and Holofernes thus describes him :—" His humour is lofty, his discourse peremptory, his tongue filed, his eye ambitious, his gait majestical, and his general behaviour vain, ridiculous, and thrasonical. He is too picked, too spruce, too affected, too odd, as it were, too peregrinate, as I may call it. He draweth out the thread of his verbosity finer than the staple of his argument." These words may be regarded as Shakspere's deliberate judgment on Marlowe, delivered at Christmas, 1597. In the scene where Armado appears "armed for Hector," the allusions are very characteristic,—"The armipotent Mars, of lances the almighty," and

> "Dos't thou infamomize me among potentates?
> Thou shalt die,"

recalls to us the observation of Sir Tophas, "Epi, prepare them to the slaughter."

The lords concealing themselves after repeating their sonnets, is probably a hint taken from Diana's nymphs in *Gallathea*, act third, scene first.

But Shakspere, by making in the gaiety of his heart an inpious onslaught on the divinity of Euphuism, and indulging also in a Bironical jest at Sir Nathaniel the curate, as *Alisander*, drew down upon himself the good humoured wrath of his old friend, who quickly gave him a Roland for his Oliver, by capping him with the ears of an ass as Midas. In this comedy there cannot be a doubt, "our pleasant Willy, the divine Williams," is the king "with asses ears." Midas is a great king and conqueror; he entertains Bacchus, and over their cups he utters a foolish wish, that every thing he touches may turn to gold; this wish Bacchus grants him, remarking at the same time he'll repent of it; he does so, and is freed from the consequences by bathing in the Pactolus; on his return from the river, passing through a wood, he is appointed judge in a musical contest, and gives the prize to Pan against Apollo; the god, irate with his folly, gives him the ears of an ass; the king in penitence goes to Greece, and offers up sacrifice at the shrine of Apollo, who releases him from his punishment. What an accurate and beautiful allegory is this of Shakspere's career up to 1589. He goes to London in 1585, is the successful author of *Pericles* and the *Two Gentlemen of Verona*; studies Latin literature, associates with the Bacchanals, and writes *Titus Andronicus* in their false and gilded style, plated with Latin; he washes out his errors in the beautiful comedy of *All's Well that Ends Well*. Again, seized with the desire of distinguishing himself in tragedy, and struck with the success of *Tamburlaine*, he mistakes Pan [Marlowe] for Apollo, and writes himself an ass in *Dido* and *Æneas*; sees his error, repents, studies the Greek dramatists, and *Hamlet* is the successful result.

This allegory is so transparent, so clear, and self-evident, we need not be at all surprised, Shakspere's commentators have never discovered it. Let us examine the comedy of *Midas* a little more minutely. After reading a few pages, the reader will not fail to notice the great similarity between the passage beginning with "my mistress' disposition" in act first, scene first, and the dialogue between Launce and Speed in the *Two Gentlemen of Verona,* act third, scene first. That this dialogue is really a jocular conversation between Shakspere and Lyly, I have all along suspected; there is so much difference of character between them;—Speed establishes his character for "a quick wit;" Launce, on the contrary, very soon earns the reputation of "a mad cap" and "an ass," and yet Launce can pun as perseveringly as Speed. An elegant critic can scarcely contain his love for Launce; he pictures to himself Shakspere in the scene between Launce and Crab as there describing his own leave-taking from Stratford. But be this as it may, in the corresponding passage in *Midas* there cannot be the slightest doubt, that Licio is Lyly, and Petulus, my dear little pet, is our pleasant Willy; Licio speaks of his blue nose and bald head, and is evidently a good ten years older than his fellow-page. It is also pleasing to note, that Lyly not only makes Petulus humorous, but even gives him the advantage over Licio in wit. Licio speaking of his nose, reminds us of the passage in *Love's Labour's Lost:*—

> *Nath.* "My scutcheon plain declares that I am Alexander.
> *Boyet.* Your nose says, no, you are not; for it stands too right.
> *Biron.* Your nose smells, no, in this, most tender-smelling knight."

The conversation between the wags and huntsman, act fourth, scene third, is a paraphrase of the second scene in the fourth act of *Love's Labour's Lost;* as Holofernes is a "Latin pedant," and knows not the language of the chase, so the Huntsman is a *"sporting pedant,"* and knows not Latin; very likely the Huntsman is Constable Dull, who blunders over "*hand credo*," and in this instance over "*fecere disertum.*" Minutius appears to be a second edition of Moth; and Licio's exclamation "*Deus bone*" can only be regarded as a direct allusion to the observation of Sir Nathaniel, "*Laus Deo bone intelligo.*" Motto's expression, " you shall have the beard, *in manner and form following,*" is of course an allusion to Costard.

To the preceding may be added the following note:—

"Orpheus harp was strung with poets' sinews."—
Two Gentlemen of Verona.

" So sweet and musical
As bright Apollo's lute strung with his hair."—
Love's Labour's Lost.

"As the sun, he is represented with golden hair, so it means with golden wire.

"The very same sort of conception occurs in Lyly's *Midas*, a play which most probably preceded Shakspere's. Act fourth, scene first. Pan tells Apollo, "Had thy lute been of lawrell, and the strings of Daphne's hair, thy tunes might have been compared to my notes."— *Warton.*

I trust the reader begins to perceive there is a very intimate connection between *Midas* and *Love's Labour's Lost*. Let us now examine into the character and deeds of King Midas. In ancient biography, Midas is represented as an effeminate king of Phrygia, and not a word about his wars or any thing of the sort; but the Midas of the comedy is no less a mighty warrior than a magnificent monarch, a constant fear and jealousy to the neighbouring potentates. We thus see, the Midas of

Lyly is no more the Midas of history, than the poetical Antony of Shakspere, is the Mark Antony of history.

Amongst other ambitious schemes, Midas is exceedingly anxious to conquer the island of Lesbos. In ancient times the island was divided into several petty republics, but in the comedy, it is ruled over by a king :—

Celthus. "More than all this, Amintas, though we dare not so much as mutter it, their king (little bald-pated John Lyly, the Fiddlestick of Oxford,) is such a one as dazzleth the clearest eyes with majesty, daunteth the valiantest hearts with courage, and for virtue filleth all the world with wonder."

The other passages in this scene refer to Shakspere's imitations of the barbarian school, as *Titus Andronicus,* and *Dido* and *Æneas* :—

"'Tis true; yet since Midas grew so mischievous, as to *blur his diadem with blood,* which should glitter with nothing but pity; "—"well then this I say, when a lion doth so much degenerate from princely kind, that he will borrow of the beasts, I say he is no lion, but a monster;—he is worthy also to have the ears of an ass."—"He seeks to conquer Lesbos," that is, Euphuism.

Midas. "Methinks there's more sweetness in the pipe of Pan, than Apollo's lute ;—What hast thou done, Apollo ? the ears of an ass upon the head of a king?—If I return to Phyrgia I shall be pointed at.—What will they say in Lesbos, if happily these news come to Lesbos? ah, foolish Midas! a just reward, for thy pride 'to wax poor, for thy overweening to wax dull, for thy ambition to wax humble. But I must see to cover my shame by art, lest being once discovered to these petty kings of Mysia, Pisidia, and Galatia, they all join to add to mine asses ears, of all the beasts the dullest, a sheep's heart, of all the beasts the fearfullest; and so cast lots for those kingdoms, that I have won with so many lives, and kept with so many envies."

The allusions in this speech are so applicable, so pertinent, they scarcely require any explanation:—"in Lesbos," at the *Mitre*;—the petty kings of Mysia, Pisidia, and Galatia, are the three dramatists, Marlowe, Peele, and Greene, proved by the initial letters; the kingdoms won with so many lives and kept with so *many envies* refer to his plays;—he also blames himself for his pride, overweening, and ambition, of which he is accused by his friends in Hamlet, and in the interview with Ophelia, Hamlet says:—

" I am myself indifferent honest,
But I could accuse myself of such crimes;
It had been better my mother had ne'er borne me,
O I am very *proud, ambitious, disdainful.*"—Ed. 1603.

It may also be here mentioned, that of the three courtiers in the opening of the play, Eristus is Peele; Martius, Marlowe; and Greene, who was the neediest of the three, is Mellacrites, who urges Midas to ask of Bacchus the golden touch; and afterwards when Martius says, "This will make Pisidia wanton, Lycaonia stiffe," we have in two words the distinctive characters of Peele and Lodge.

On the king's return, his courtiers remark:—

Erist. " I marvel what Midas meaneth to be *so melancholy*, since his hunting.
Mel. It is a good word in Midas, otherwise I should term it in another blockishness. Methinks he seemeth *so jealous* of us all, and becomes so overthwart to all others, that either I must conjecture *his wits are not his own*, or *his meaning very hard to some.*"
[*The Reeds.* Midas of Phrygia hath asses ears.]
Erist. This is monstrous and either portends *some mischief to the king*, or unto *the state confusion.*"

The reader will readily perceive, how pointedly all this refers to Hamlet:—

> *Hor.* "This bodes some *strange eruption* to our state.
> *Ham.* My father's spirit in arms! all is not well;
> I doubt *some foul play*."

The following advice from Apollo perhaps alludes to Shakspere's quarrel with Nash and Greene, and also shows, that Lyly felt hurt at the practical joke in *Love's Labour's Lost*:—

> *Apollo.* "Then attend Midas,
> Let thy head be glad of one crown,
> And take care to keep one friend."

How pertinently does this last line apply to Shakspere; whilst it is scarcely applicable to the king, whose courtiers and subjects are most faithful and obedient, and deeply grieved at his misfortune, particularly his barber Motto:—

> *Motto.* "I tell you, boys, it is melancholy that now troubleth me."

But who is Motto, and who is Dello, his boy? The following observation of Petulus must refer to Greene's beard, of which Nash tells us, "a jolly long red peake like the spire of a steeple he (Greene) cherisht continually without cutting, whereat a man might hang a jewel, it was so sharp and pendant":—

> *Pet.* "And here I vow by my concealed beard, if ever it chance to be discovered to the world, that it may make a pike-devant. I will have it so sharp pointed, that it shall stab Motto like a poynado."

and again we read:—

Pet. " Ah; a bots on the barber! ever since I cozened him of the golden beard, I have had the tooth-ache.

Motto. I did but rub his gums, and presently the rheum evaporated.

Licio. Deus bone, is that word come into the barber's basin."—Act iii., scene 2.

Here is clear confirmation, or rather anticipation, of Greene's words in 1592, " an upstart crow beautified with our feathers;" but whatever the theft may have been, it is certain, both Lyly and Shakspere laugh at it as a capital joke. Greene's charge is thus brought down to something that occurred before the appearance of *Hamlet;* consequently it can only have reference to *Titus Andronicus* and the *Two Gentlemen of Verona.* As Greene had been in Spain, it is possible Shakspere may have taken lessons from him in Spanish, and may have appropriated some passages from the *Diana of Montemayor,* which Greene may have been translating for one of his own novels; and in the song at the end of the scene are the lines :—

Pet. " O what will rid me of this pain?
Motto. Some pellitory fetcht from Spain."

It thus appears, that Motto is Greene; and Dello says, "if I durst tell the truth, as lusty as I am here, I lie upon a bed of beards; a bots of their bristles, and they that owe them, they are harder than flocks." This observation refers to Nash's position in 1589; what with the Marprelate controversy and his quarrel with Shakspere as well as with Greene and Lyly, whom he abuses in his *Anatomie of Absurditie,* he may well be said to " lie upon a bed of beards;" and we may be sure, Lyly, would pay off old scores and make a ridiculous puppet of him in this comedy;—also the question of Petulus, "yea Motto hast thou Latin," is perhaps an allusion to Nash's *Epistle* prefixed to Greene's *Menaphon*. Nash in writing this *Epistle* acted as Greene's assistant, and thus stood in the same relative position to him, as Dello to Motto.

We may then sum up,—Midas and Shakspere are identical, as regards the golden touch, the ears of an ass, the attack on Lesbos or Euphuism, and the journey to Greece.

Act first, scene second, refers to act third, scene first, in the *Two Gentlemen of Verona*.

Act fourth, scene third, refers to act fourth, scene second, in *Love's Labour's Lost*.

And the observation of Eristus, "this is monstrous, and either portends some mischief to the king or unto the state confusion," refers to *Hamlet*.

Licio and Petulus are Lyly and Shakspere;

Motto and Dello are Greene and Nash;

and it should be particularly noticed, that Martius (Marlowe) is the only character that speaks uniformly with disrespect of Apollo; and in the last scene, Midas speaks severely, though pertinently, to him:—

Mid. "Thou art barbarous, not valiant. No more, Martius, I am the learned'st in Phrygia to interpret these oracles."

In reading these two beautiful comedies, *Endymion* and *Midas*, at the name of Shakspere all difficulties vanish, the curtain of night is rent, and daylight pours in; his name is the watchword, the "open sesame," Aladdin's lamp.

Lyly wrote another comedy, *Mother Bombie*, apparently in a combative spirit, as a trial of ingenuity *versus* the *Comedy of Errors*.

On examining how the account stands between Shakspere and Lyly during the five years from 1586 to 1590, both inclusive, it is evident from the foregoing analysis, the balance must be credited to Shakspere, and somewhat heavily; yet I should be sorry to make the same charges against Lyly as have been made against Shakspere. These resemblances are not, on either side, to be regarded as petty thefts or stolen ideas, but as complimentary allusions, delightful reminiscences; when Shakspere wrote Dogberry and his watchmen, and the Fairies pinching Falstaff, how could he avoid remembering the watchmen that guarded, and the Fairies that kissed Endymion? Dear, good old Lyly! yet thou liest on the library-shelf unthumbed, for the novel-reader understandeth thee not.

But, it seems, during the next twenty years Midas makes frequent and terrific raids into the dominions of the Lesbian king, and spite of all his valiant bees, wasp-like, steals away the honey:—

> " Hark, the lark at heaven's gate sings,
>   And Phœbus 'gins arise."

"Shakspere was familiar with his works, and paraphrases some of his best passages. He was certainly one of those authors Greene accused him so bitterly of copying. In the notes to these volumes, many such passages are pointed out, and others may readily be added. Such and so many resemblances could not be accidental."

I trust it has been clearly shown, that up to the year

1590, the borrowings from Lyly have been of the most trivial kind; and it is just possible, that Shakspere, acting the part of Apelles at the Blackfriars in 1585, was pleased with the phrase, " stars are to be look'd, not reached at," as a concise turn of his own thoughts :—

Ant. " Her face, like heaven, enticeth thee to view
A countless glory, which desert must gain :
And which, without desert, because thine eye
Presumes to reach, all thy whole heap must die."—
Pericles, act i., scene 1.

Thaisa. " And the device he bears upon his shield
Is a black Æthiop, reaching at the sun."—
Act ii., scene 2.

Let us now make a further examination, and take a closer view of poor, despised Pericles. Like Hamlet, he is of a tender and sensitive disposition, melancholy, and apt to soliloquize. To the valuable notice on the authenticity of Pericles, in the *Pictorial Shakspere*, may be added the following resemblances; after reading the riddle Pericles says :—

" Sharp physick is the last ; "

and Hamlet, on seeing his uncle praying,

" This physick but prolongs thy sickly days ; "

and again,

Sim. " What do you think, Sir, of my daughter ?
Per. As of a most virtuous princess."—
Pericles, act ii., scene 5.

Cor. "My lord, what doe you thinke of me?
King. As of a true friend, and a most loving subject."—
Hamlet, ed. 1603.

Antiochus is evidently the same individual as Claudius, and the similarity is still more distinctly marked in the first sketch of *Hamlet;* each is guilty of incest, and in each there is the same energy and decision of character, and in each the same dread or fear:—

Ant. "He hath found the meaning, for the which we mean
To have his head.
And therefore instantly this prince must die.
It fits thee not to ask the reason why,
Because we bid it.
Thaliard, adieu! till Pericles be dead,
My heart can lend no succour to my head."—
Pericles.

King. "To England is he gone, ne'er to return:
Our letters are unto the King of England,
That on the sight of them, on his allegiance,
He presently without demanding why,
That Hamlet lose his head, for he must die,
There's more in him than shallow eyes can see:
He once being dead, why then our state is free."—
Hamlet, ed. 1603.

The dialogue between Pericles and the fishermen, strongly reminds us of Hamlet and the clowns in the churchyard; in fact, the two scenes may be regarded as essentially the same in spirit and meaning:—

2 *Fish.* "Canst thou catch any fishes then?
Per. I never practised it.
2 *Fish.* Nay, then thou wilt starve sure; for here's nothing to be got now-a-days, unless thou canst *fish* for 't."—
Pericles, act ii., scene 1.

Here we have the very pun in *Hamlet* :—

Cor. "Now my good lord, do you know me?
Ham. Yea, very well; y' are a *fishmonger*."

Hamlet calls him a fishmonger because he is trying to *fish out* his secret.

From these extracts it is manifest, these two plays were intimately connected in the poet's mind; and if there be any truth in the critical theory about germs and pre-existent states, we shall find the difference between Pericles and Hamlet is so much and no more; the one is an apothecary's apprentice just "out of his indentures," going up to London to walk the hospitals; the other is the same individual, three years older, a Licentiate of the Apothecaries' Company, and a Member of the Royal College of Surgeons; a young gentleman extremely well satisfied with himself, very decided and off-hand, no fear of a ghost, and rather apt to quiz and mock old Dr. Polonius. It is worthy of note, these extracts are all taken from the first two acts, which are supposed to bear the fewest traces of Shakspere's hand.

Mr. Armitage Brown observes, "From the moment Marina appears, Shakspere takes her by the hand and leads her gently onward;" it is pleasing to see the young lady has at least one friend amongst these critics; her expression, "My heart leaps to be gone into my mother's bosom," is similar to Iphigenia's exclamation on seeing her father :—

"My father to thy arms I wish to run
Clasp'd to thy bosom;"—*Iphigenia in Aulis.*

most probably the resemblance is accidental. Unfortunately for Mr. Brown's judgment, he further observes, " but I cannot perceive he (Shakspere) had any connection with the vile crew who surround her." This is the point, the critics and commentators having so lamentably misunderstood; the poet selected the tale from old Gower as harmonizing completely with his own poetical conception about Tellus and Cynthia; the play is essentially a Hymn to Diana, the goddess of chastity and sister of Apollo, the god " of poesie and physicke." In contrast to virgin innocence and the purity of the married life, the apothecary's apprentice gives a medical view of the mysteries of the temple of Venus; however coarse the scenes may be, they have entirely a moral tendency, and were, apparently, not objected to in those days, since the play was a popular favourite for many years; and however coarse, they are far less lewd and prurient than several passages in Lyly's first comedy, the *Woman in the Moon*, and which, we know, was performed in the presence of the Virgin Queen, " as it was presented before her Highness."

From the preceding statements it would appear, Shakspere went to London in 1585, taking *Pericles* with him; brings out the *Two Gentlemen of Verona* in the spring, and *Titus Andronicus* in the autumn, '86; *All's Well that Ends Well* in the spring, and *Dido and Æneas* in the autumn, '87; being then deeply distressed at the rejection of his tragedy, he meditates and studies long and earnestly over the next; and in consequence of being also much occupied with his duties as Captain of the Theatrical Volunteers, *Hamlet,* the crowning glory of that ever-memorable year, 1588, does not make its appearance till just before Christmas; then Shakspere pours forth the exuberance of his joy in *Love's Labour's Lost,* followed by that unrivalled farce, the *Comedy of Errors,* in the autumn of 1589.

That our pleasant Willy shortly afterwards rusticated himself, bolted into country quarters, frighted by the false fire of Nash's caustic *Epistle* and by the Kentish fire of Lyly's humourous comedy, can scarcely be credited; but it rests on indubitable authority, that he did not make his sacrificial offering to Apollo publicly in the year 1590, or only just before Christmas. It appears, London was at this time rent with religious dissensions and controversies, and the stage transformed into a theological cock-pit. Spenser has so beautifully and so accurately described this unfortunate period, that I cannot do better than quote his lines from the *Tears of the Muses,* where Thalia thus laments:—

> "And he, the man whom Nature self had made
>   To mock herself, and truth to imitate.
> With kindly counter, under mimic shade,
>   Our pleasant Willy, ah! is dead of late;
> With whom all joy and jolly merriment
> Is also deaded, and in dolour drent.
>
> "Instead thereof, scoffin scurrility,
>   And scorning folly with contempt is crept,
> Rolling in rimes of shameless ribaudry,
>   Without regard, or due decorum kept;
> Each idle wit at will presumes to make,
> And doth the learned's task upon him take.

> "But that same gentle spirit, from whose pen
>   Large streams of honey and sweet nectar flow,
>   Scorning the boldness of such base-born men,
>   Which dare their follies forth so rashly throw,
>   Doth rather choose to sit in idle cell,
>   Than so himself to mockery to sell."

But Spenser here makes, happily, in one sense, a slight mistake, Shakspere *did not* " choose to sit in idle cell;" we now know, he was hard at work, studying the *Chronicles* of Hall and Holinshed; and that his brains, like swallows in busy consultation before winging their flight across the ocean, were deeply pondering over the whole sweep of his historical plays, the great English *Iliad.* Yet it would appear from the testimony of eminent authorities, that he actually wrote only one play, *Romeo and Juliet,* between Christmas 1589, and Christmas 1592; during these three years, *Endymion,* from some unknown cause, must have fallen asleep; but it is questionable whether the chloroform of the enchanting goddess operated on Shakspere or on his commentators. Mr. C. Knight has, with great ability, argued in favour of Shakspere's claim to *Henry VI.*, and the *Two Parts of the Contention,* now called the *Three Parts of Henry VI.* So conclusive, so irrefragable are his arguments, I must refer the reader, who would study the subject, to his admirable *Essay on Henry VI. and Richard III.*

I have used the term *English Iliad* advisedly; for I feel confident Shakspere intended all these plays to be so regarded; the youthful poet here measures himself with Homer, as he had previously with the dramatists of Greece; and this assertion is based on the opening of

Henry VI., which is the first in order of composition, as well as the first of a sequence forming a perfect epic poem.

If the Reverend Mr. Hunter can say, "there is something very Greekish in this:"—

Portia. "I stand for sacrifice,
　　　The rest aloof are the Dardanian wives
　　　With bleared visages, come forth to view
　　　The issue of the exploit."—*Merchant of Venice.*

it may with equal truth be said, there is something very Homeric in this :—

War.　　　"This brawl to-day
　　　Grown to this faction, in the Temple garden,
　　　Shall send, between the red rose and the white,
　　　A thousand souls to death and deadly night."—
　　　　　　　　Henry VI., act ii., scene 4.

and it may be added, Shakspere has given us in the first and third scenes of the first act, a better translation than either Cowper, Pope, or Chapman, of the first book of the *Iliad;* for it is literally a *translation;* the jars between Gloster and Winchester reminding us of Agamemnon and Achilles.

It is a remarkable circumstance, that in *Hamlet*, the story of which resembles the story of Orestes, there should be a paraphrase, or rather, a scene with quotations from a scene in the *Electra of Sophocles*, and in *Henry VI.*, the commencement of a dramatic epic, we have a paraphrase of the first book of the *Iliad;*—nor can I resist the impression, so strong a mesmeric and spirit-rapping hold it has on my imagination, that the line, "the bad revolting stars, *That have concented unto Henry's death,*" is a Shaksperian translation of the Homeric phrase, "such was the will of Jove;" that the one gave rise to the other;—nor should it be overlooked, that the jar commences in *Henry VI.* by Gloster's angry reply to Winchester, just as in the *Iliad* by Agamemnon's haughty conduct to the priest Chryses; and the parallel may be carried still farther, since all the mishaps to the Greeks arose from Agamemnon's taking Brisëis from Achilles, and the real cause of the Contention begins with Plantaganet's claim to the Dukedom of York in the Temple garden; and whilst in *Hamlet* the revenge is Greek, in these plays the warriors, no less cruel than abusive, are essentially Homeric both in their language and actions.*

Had these resemblances occurred in other plays, they might have been regarded as accidental, but as the case stands, such a supposition is inadmissible;—for my part, I believe Shakspere read the Greek authors in their own language; but however that may be, these facts deserve the serious consideration of those parties, who are of opinion, Shakspere was as ignorant as Nash and tradition would make him.

It is possible, *Henry VI.*, like *Henry V.*, may have been preceded by an elder play, equally "*contemptible*" with the *Famous Victories;* but of such a play having ever existed, there is not the slightest trace or evidence, excepting in the inequalities of the play itself, which may reasonably be accounted for by its having been an early production.

---

* Maginn considers the character of Ulysses in *Troilus and Cressida*, "to be a studied antagonism" to the *Ulysses* of Homer; and, he adds, "at all events I think it would not be far short of a miracle, if Shakspere had not read in some language the *Iliad* and *Odyssey.*" —*Fraser's Magazine*, Sept. 1839, p. 270.

These plays, *Henry VI.* and the two parts of the *Contention,* must have followed one another in rapid succession, and were probably brought out early in 1591, and *Richard III.* the following Christmas, or in the spring of 1592.

Besides these plays, forming an harmonious whole or second half of the English *Iliad, Romeo and Juliet* was produced within the same period, in 1591. It has been said, Shakspere's heroines do not set a very good example, as nearly all make runaway matches; but how are they rewarded? If those parties who carp and rail at Shakspere as a writer, having no moral object in view, would read and understand, they would cease such idle revilings. In this very play does he set up Juliet as an example or a warning to the boarding-school Misses in their teens? Is she not a most affectionate and enthusiastic young lady, so that everyone pities and regrets her misfortunes? but are they not the consequences of her own misconduct? she mystifies her parents, and instead of pouring her griefs into the bosom of her mother, she goes to her father-confessor, and thus the poet shows how injurious is the influence of the Popish priest; and further, how assuredly young lovers are punished for yielding to their wilful and unbridled passions. What a contrast is this wilful, forward, black-eyed minx to the sweet Ophelia, so dutiful and so loving; whose affections are far more pure, and whose love is equally intense. Both perish; but how far greater are the trials of Ophelia, and how far more hopeless is her case than Juliet's. Her father murdered by her lover, he banished and a lunatic; and whilst

Juliet brings her own miseries on herself by want of candour to her parents, Ophelia is sacrificed through the crotchety idea of Hamlet pretending to be cracked. "Juliet plays most of her pranks," says Johnson, "under the appearance of religion; perhaps Shakspere meant to punish her hypocrisy." Is not that the character of an Italian, rather than an English maiden?

We have now arrived at a very interesting period in the life of Shakspere. Shortly before Christmas, 1592, or early in the following spring, were produced two comedies, the *Merry Wives of Windsor* and *Midsummer Night's Dream*. There is a tale, that the first was composed in the course of a fortnight by command of her Majesty; but her Majesty's commands must have been limited to the writing of a comedy, as she could have known nothing about Falstaff, since *Henry IV*. was not produced till several years later. Most probably the comedy was written in the autumn, as the German Duke, who visited Windsor, received his passport from Lord Howard, September 2nd, 1592.

In the two parts of *Henry IV*. the character of Falstaff is drawn with inimitable skill, and Sir John may truly say, "I am myself alone;" but in the *Merry Wives of Windsor* we see our pleasant Willy in the guise of the fat knight, like a pretty mischievous child peeping from behind a mask, laughing and making merry with his old friend Lyly as Sir Hugh Evans; and at the same time Marlowe, our old acquaintance Sir Tophas, Parolles, and Don Armado, is again caricatured under the name of Pistol.

Let us make an examination into the various allusions and resemblances, and see how far these assertions are borne out:—

Fal. "Remember, Jove, thou wast a bull for thy Europa. You were also, Jupiter, a swan for the love of Leda. O, Jove, a beastly fault! and then another fault in the semblance of a fowl; think on't, Jove; a foul fault."—

Act v., scene 5.

Apel. "This is Europa. This is Leda, whom Jove deceived in likeness of a swan.

Camp. A fair woman, but a foul deceit."—

Campaspe, act iii., scene 3.

Falstaff then lies down [like Corsites in *Endymion*, around whom "the Fairies daunce and with a song pinch him;"] a similar direction is given *in the old quartos*, says Theobald, "during this song they pinch him" (Falstaff).

On rising up Falstaff says:—

Fal. "I do begin to perceive that I am made an ass.

Ford. Ay, and an ox too; both the proofs are extant."

It is very evident Falstaff has made an ass of himself; but what does Ford mean by "*Ay, and an ox too;*" how could he, a burgher of Windsor, add, "both the proofs are extant;" when Falstaff had on the antlers of "a Windsor stag," and not the horns of an ox? Perhaps the following extract from the comedy of *Midas* may throw some light on the subject:—

Mid. "What hast thou done, Apollo? the ears of an ass on the head of a king? Help, Pan! or Midas perisheth.

> *Pan.* I cannot undo what Apollo hath done, nor give thee any amends, unless to those ears thou wilt have added these horns.
>
> 1. *Nymph.* It were very well, that it might be hard to judge, whether he were more ox or ass.
>
> *Apollo.* Farewell, Midas.
>
> *Pan.* Midas, farewell."

Ford's observation, "Ay, and an ox too," thus becomes proof irresistible,—Shakspere was Midas, and that he enjoyed the joke.

> *Fal.* "Am I ridden with a Welch goat too.
>
> Secse and putter! have I lived to stand at the taunts of one that makes fritters of English.
>
> I am not able to answer the Welch flannel; ignorance itself is a plummet o'er me; use me as you will."

These jests refer to Euphuism; the author of *Euphues* being transformed into a Welshman; and in *Love's Labour's Lost* the Princess says of Don Armado:—

> "He speaks not like a man of God's making."

From these allusions to three of Lyly's comedies, *Campaspe, Endymion,* and *Midas,* all in one scene, it may be reasonably inferred, Shakspere himself is laughing behind the back of the fat old knight; for it is highly improbable he would have made these allusions so direct and pointed without some definite object and meaning.

The observation, "Fery goot; I will make a prief of it in my note-book," directly connects Sir Hugh Evans with Sir Nathaniel in *Love's Labour's Lost*:—

> *Nath.* "A most singular and choice epithet."—
>
> [*Takes out his table-book.*

And we are strongly reminded of Costard's character of Sir Nathaniel by Sir Hugh's behaviour in the field, whilst waiting for Dr. Caius, where he shows such a tender and generous disposition without detracting from his personal courage.

Sir Hugh's remark, "for divers philosophers hold, that the lips is parcel of the mouth," is a complimentary allusion to a passage in *Midas*; and his examination of William in Latin, has reference to another passage in the same scene :—

> *Licio.* "Thou servest Mellacrites, and I his daughter; which is the better man?
> *Pet.* The masculine gender is more worthy than the feminine."

It has been previously shown, that Licio is Lyly, and Petulus Shakspere; and here we have Sir Hugh questioning a little boy called William, and at the end of the examination his mother says :—

> *Mrs. P.* "He is a better scholar than I thought he was.
> *Evans.* He is a good sprag memory."

If the other allusions hold good, it must also be granted, Shakspere here directly asserts, he is a better scholar than the world gives him credit for.

As for Pistol, there can be no doubt about him; he is a braggart, a tame cheater, and in his way a learned man, making quotations chiefly from Marlowe's and Lyly's works, and so identifying himself :—

> *Slend.* "If I be drunk, I'll be drunk with those, that have the fear of God, and not with drunken knaves.
> *Pist.* How now Mephistophilus?
> *Bard.* Like three German devils, three Doctor Faustus's.

Pist. Thou art the Mars of malecontents.
Let vultures gripe thy guts!*
O, base Gongarian wight! wilt thou the spigot wield?†
He loves thy gallimawfry, Ford, perpend.‡

The following points evidently refer to Sir Tophas' description of his beboved Dipsas in *Endymion*:—

Fal. "My honest lads, I will tell you what I am about.
Pist. Two yards and more.
Fal. No quips now, Pistol; indeed I am in the waist two yards about; but I am now about no waste, I am about thrift.
Pist. As many devils entertain; and, "*To her boy*," say I.
Fal. Sometimes the beam of her view gilded my foot, sometimes my portly belly.
Pist. Then did the sun on dunghill shine."§—

Act i., scene 3.

Top. "What a low stature she is, and yet what a great foot she carrieth! How thrifty must she be in whom there is no waste! How virtuous is she like to be, over whom no man can be jealous!"

"There appeared in my sleep a goodly owl, who sitting upon my shoulder, cried twit, twit, and before my eyes presented herself the express image of Dipsas. I marvailed what the owl said, till at the last, I perceived twit, twit, to it, to it; only by contraction admonished by this vision, to make account of my sweet Venus."—*Endymion*, act iii., scene 3.

Pist. "Shall I Sir Pandarus of Troy become
        And by my side wear steel? then Lucifer take all!"

At this very time Marlowe was acting the part of a

---

* "A burlesque on a passage in Tamburlaine."—*Stevens*.

† This is a parody on "A base Gongarian, wilt thou the distaff wield?"

‡ This is perhaps a ridicule on a passage in the old comedy of *Cambyses*, "my sapient words I say perpend."—*Stevens*.

§ A quotation from *Euphues*, "The sun shineth upon a dunghill."

needy flatterer and sycophant to the young Earl of Southampton.

As Pistol's "two yards and more" is not an original witticism, we may feel certain,—"the world's mine oyster, which I with sword will open" is also borrowed, perhaps a joke of Shakspere's or Lyly's over their oysters at the *Mitre*;—Pistol is not represented here as a wit, but rather as a *learned* man, all his bright sayings are quotations.

The above statement, containing so many allusions and resemblances to passages in *Endymion* and *Midas*, forms a mass of evidence, which forces on us the conclusion, that Pistol, like Sir Tophas, is a caricature of Marlowe; that Sir Hugh Evans is a Welch portrait of Lyly; and that Shakspere is acting the part of Sir John Falstaff, enjoying the fun, and very discreetly putting the buck's horns upon his own head to save himself from a worse fate, the good-humoured wrath of the monarch of Lesbos.

It must then also be granted, Shakspere acknowledges the truth of Shallow's accusation:—

Shal. "Knight, you have beaten my men, killed my deer, and broke open my lodge.
Fal. But not kiss'd your keeper's daughter?
Shal. Tut, a pin! this shall be answer'd.
Fal. I will answer it straight;—I have done all this:—That is now answered."

A deal of nonsensical cant has been uttered against Shakspere on this score; but it is now acknowledged, "Deer-stealing in Shakspere's day was regarded only as a youthful frolic, &c." *Staunton's Shakspere*.

But the most interesting part of the comedy remains yet to be examined into; we have mentioned a little boy, named William, but there is also a young lady named Anne; now if the preceding observations be admitted, it follows as a matter of course, that sweet Anne Page stands as the representative of Anne Hathaway; and Master Fenton, of the apothecary's apprentice, William Shakspere. The evidence in their favour is as clear and strong as that which has been advanced with regard to the other characters. "In fact we do know," says Drake, "that Shakspere married for love, but we do not know of any the smallest intimation or hint, previous to the wild conjecture of Oldys, that coldness or estrangement had subsisted between the poet and his wife." Much ink has been spilt about his unhappiness in having married a lady older than himself, and the proofs after ransacking his plays, are the lines in *Twelfth Night*, a couple of lines in *Midsummer Night's Dream*, and the acute remark of Sir Hugh Evans, "I like not when a 'oman has a great peard; I spy a great peard under her muffler."

It seems singular and not very creditable to human nature, that such illiberal surmises should have been drawn from the lines in *Twelfth Night* and so much harped upon; whilst, as far as I am aware, no notice whatever has been taken of the marriage of Master Fenton and Miss Anne Page:—

> *Host.* "What say you to young Master Fenton? he capers, he dances, he has eyes of youth, he writes verses, he speaks holiday, he smells April and May; he will carry 't he will carry 't; 'tis in his buttons; he will carry 't.

Page. Not by my consent I promise you. The gentleman is of no having; he kept company with the wild Prince and Poins; he is of too high a region, he knows too much. No, he shall not knit a knot in his fortunes with the finger of my substance: if he take her let him take her simply; the wealth I have waits on my consent, and my consent goes not that way."—Act iii., scene 2.

Anne. Gentle Master Fenton,
    Yet seek my father's love; still seek it, sir:
    If opportunity and humblest suit
    Cannot attain it, why then.—Hark you hither."
                    [*They converse apart.*

Fent. " You do amaze her: Hear the truth of it.
    You would have married her most shamefully,
    Where there was no proportion held in love.
    The truth is, she and I, long since contracted,
    Are now so sure that nothing can dissolve us.
    The offence is holy, that she hath committed;
    And this deceit looses the name of craft,
    Of disobedience or unduteous title;
    Since therein she doth evitate and shun
    A thousand irreligious cursed hours,
    Which forced marriage would have brought upon her."

How closely and accurately do all these circumstances fit in with Shakspere's own marriage; probably a run-a-way match without the knowledge of their parents. How pleasingly does the host describe the youthful poet, ascribing to him the very sins which Goodman Hathaway would most object to,—he dances, writes verses, and speaks holiday. Is it not also possible and probable, that the daughter, according to tradition, "eminently beautiful," remained in a state of single blessedness till her twenty-fifth year, because she would not marry, where she did not love; and as Justice

Shallow is acknowledged to have been a Lucy of Charlecote, it is possible, cousin Slender and Dr. Cains may both have been rejected admirers of that "splendid gal" Anne Hathaway, the prototype probably of Thaisa and Silvia. Moreover, Master Fenton's address occurs just at the end of the play, and is delivered with so much earnestness, and the lines are so peculiarly appropriate to Shakspere's own marriage, we are necessitated to believe, they are the genuine utterances of his own mind, and that his own marriage had consequently been a very happy one; and that all the circumstances connected with the previous contract or betrothal, *" long since contracted,"* had been reputable and consonant with the feelings of persons in their station :—

"The offence is holy that she hath committed,"

This analysis of the comedy according to "my humour," instead of detracting from the merriment of the *Merry Wives of Windsor*, adds richness and raciness to the story. No reader will ever confound the living characters of the comedy with their prototypes or shadows; and though the poet has made the marriage of Master Fenton and sweet Anne Page a vehicle for the justification of his own early marriage, yet surely they will live immortal and distinct from our pleasant Willy and his own sweet Anne.—Mr. Halliwell has pointed out, that Sly, Herne, Horne, Brome, Page, and Ford, are names found in MSS. in the Council Chamber, at Stratford.

We must now have a few minutes conversation with Thomas Nash, as he furnishes additional evidence, that Shakspere and Midas are one; and also explains a Falstaffian phrase, that has caused the shedding of much ink. The following extracts are all taken from Mr. Collier's edition of *Pierce Penniless*. Mr. Collier observes, " It seems evident that Nash felt, in the opening of the preceding epistle, (which we give literatim) that he was performing a task; but, towards the conclusion, he freed himself from this impression, and shook off the restraint upon his pen. It is impossible at this time of day to explain some of the temporary, and designedly ambiguous touches at authors of his day, near the close, but the hit at Peele and his *Tale of Troy*, 1589, seems pretty obvious, and Nash sets out with an obscure reference to Greene, and to the manner in which he was accustomed to vaunt his University Degrees at Oxford and Cambridge, in the title-pages of his tracts."

The prefatory epistle to Nash's edition of *Astrophel and Stella*, 1591, above referred to, contains the following passages :—

"Gentlemen, that have seen a thousand lines of folly drawn forth *ex uno puncto impudentiæ*, and two famous mountains to go to the conception of one mouse; that have had your ears deafened with the echo of Fames brazen towers, when only they have been toucht with a leaden pen; that have seen Pan sitting in his bower of delight, and a number of Midasses to admire his miserable hornpipes, let not your surfeited sight, new come from such puppet play, think scorn to turn aside into this theatre of pleasure."

These allusions refer to Greene, Shakspere, and Lyly; —the two universities going to form one Greene;— Fame's brazen towers and the leaden pen to Shakspere's *Henry VI.*;—and Lyly is the author of *Midas*. This explanation is confirmed by the following passage:—

" Apollo hath resigned his ivory harp unto Astrophel, and he, like Mercury, must lull you asleep with his musick. Sleep Argus, sleep Ignorance, sleep Impudence, for Mercury hath Io, and only Io Pæan belongeth to Astrophel." The name of Argus is peculiarly applicable to Lyly; Impudence is of course Greene, and Mr, Ignorance can answer for himself.

We can now also readily understand the drift of Falstaff's expression, " ignorance itself is a plummet o'er me;" evidently an allusion to this epistle. The worthy knight quibbles on the word *plummet*, a pen or lead, that is, "*a leaden pen*;" as if he had said, " I am not able to answer the Welch flannel; Nash even may abuse or jest over me; use me as you will."

The reader, on being aware that *Euphues* was published in 1580, and *Astrophel and Stella* not till 1591, though written several years before, will readily understand the following humourous piece of satire, or Dello's revenge for his ridiculous position in *Midas*; *ignis fatuus* is an admirable and most apposite name for *Euphues*, and "arise out of dunghilles" refers to the line in *Euphues*.

" The sun shineth upon a dunghill."

" The sun for a time may mask his golden head in a cloud, yet in the end the thick veil doth vanish, and his embellished blandishment appears. Long hath Astrophel (England's sun) withheld the beams of his spirit from the common view of our dark sense, and night hath hovered over the gardens of the Nine Sisters, while *ignis fatuus,* and gross fatty flames, (such as commonly arise out of dunghills) have took occasion, in the middest eclipse of his shining perfections, to wander abroad with a wisp of paper at their tails, like hobgoblins, and lead men up and down in a circle of absurdity a whole week, and never know where they are."

The following points apply to Marlowe, Shakspere, and Peele; evidently Dello is in a very uncomfortable and bristling humour if not "on a bed of beards," a hedgehog to himself as well as to his friends;—"Nor hath my prose any skill to imitate the almond leaf verse, or sit tabring five years together nothing but to bee, to bee on a paper drum."

"Others are so hardly bested for loading, that they are fain to retail the cinders of *Troy,* and the shivers of broken trunchions to fill up their boat, that else should go empty."

The "almond leaf verse" is an ironical compliment; as the second part of *Tamburlaine* and the first three books of the *Fairy Queen* were published in 1590, the public immediately discovered, that Marlowe had purloined from Spenser the passage in *Tamburlaine* commencing with:—

"Like to an almond-tree y-mounted high."

The following graphic and invaluable caricature belongs to Mr. Ignorance and no mistake :—

"An asse is no great statesman in the beastes commonwealth, though he weare his ears *upsevant muffe*, after the Muscovy fashion, and hange the lip like a capcase halfe open, or looke as demurely as a sixpenny browne loafe, for he hath some imperfections that do keep him from the common councel: yet of many he is deemed a very vertuous member, and one of the honestest sort of men that are; so that our opinion (as Sextus Empedocles) gives the name of good or ill to every thing. Out of whose works [latelie translated into English for the benefit of unlerned writers] &c."

The words, "a very vertuous member and one of the honestest sort of men," correspond remarkably with Chettle's account written in the following year, "he had himself seen his demeanour, no less civil than he excellent in the quality he professed: besides divers of worship have reported his uprightness of dealing, which argues his honesty."

In vol. ii., p. 10. of the *Shakspere Society*, is an account of Shakspere's bust; "The forehead is as fine as Raphael's or Bacon's, and the form of the nose and exquisite refinement of the mouth, with its amiable genial hilarity of wit and goodnature, so characteristic, *unideal*; bearing truth in every curve, with a little bit of the teeth shewing at the moment of smiling, which must have been often seen by those, who had the happiness to know Shakspere, and must have been pointed out to the sculptor as necessary to likeness when he was dead. The whole bust is stamped with an air of fidelity, perfectly invaluable."

The reader cannot fail to notice the singular coincidence between "hange the lip like a capcase half open," and "a little bit of the teeth shewing."

Mr. Collier, in his remarks on *Pierce Penniless*, observes, "Nash had by this time found a patron; possibly the Earl of Southampton, to whom Nash dedicates several tracts, was the nobleman intended." This appears highly probable, for "Iove's eagle-born Ganimede" can only be a young nobleman of singular beauty. Nash at this time was in great distress, and apparently dependent on the liberality of Lord Southampton, who idolized and worshipped Shakspere. Nash therefore changed his tune, and sycophant-like fawned on the mighty dramatist. In the commencement of *Pierce Penniless*, he writes:—

"Without redresse complaynes my careless verse,
And Midas eares relent not at my moane;"

and in his epistle to the printer, in the second edition, he indignantly repudiates Greene's tract as "a scald, trivial, lying pamphlet."

Since "the two parts of the *Contention* were produced as early, if not earlier, than 1591, by universal admission," the play of *Henry VI.*, alluded to by Nash in this tract, and performed at the *Rose* for the first time, March 3, 1592, must have been an imitation of Shakspere's, and probably owed its success to the principal character being performed by Alleyn, to the popularity of the subject, and to the circumstance of English troops being then in France assisting the King of Navarre, and which was perhaps one inducement why Shakspere began his historical series with *Henry VI.*

As Nash, in *Pierce Penniless*, speaks of his "beardless

years," I may mention, he was then in his twenty-fifth year, he was born in November, 1567; Marlowe in February, and Shakspere in April, 1564; Lyly in 1554, and Greene probably in 1550.

As Marlowe died on June 1, 1593, we may take this opportunity of reviewing his career as connected with Shakspere. *Tamburlaine*, it is supposed, was produced (both parts) in 1586, and, no doubt, some other play by his hand had previously appeared [let it be remembered the two poets are exactly of the same age]; thus it becomes dubious, whether the palm of priority should be given to Shakspere or Marlowe; but as Shakspere went straight to London to join the Blackfriars Company, it may reasonably be supposed, his thoughts had long been turned to the stage, and that he had consequently written a play previous to *Pericles*. As *Arden of Feversham* cannot be attributed to any known author anterior to 1592, surely the supposition is admissible, that it was the work on which Shakspere tried his "prentice hand;" apart from the opinion of German critics, it is strong presumptive evidence thereof, that the clear and cautious judgment of Mr. C. Knight apparently leans to a similar supposition. Though a domestic tragedy, it it composed decidedly on Endymion's theory, the young Swan beats his wings vigorously, eager to have a snap at the moon:—

"The character of Black Will is drawn with great force, but there is probably something of a youthful judgment in making the murderer speak in high poetry. The characters and events are lifted out of ordinary life of purpose by the poet. The ambition of a young writer may have carried this too far, but the principle upon which he worked was a right one. He aimed to produce something higher than a literal copy of every-day life, and this constitutes the essential distinction between *Arden of Feversham* and the *Yorkshire Tragedy*, as between Shakspere and Heywood."—*Pictorial Shakspere*.

Even if it be not conceded that *Arden of Feversham* was written by Shakspere, still he claims precedence of Marlowe as a playwright.

It may then be taken for granted, the two parts of *Tamburlaine* appeared in 1586, *Faustus* at Christmas, '87, and the *Jew of Malta* at Christmas, '89, or early in 1590. Let any person read *Tamburlaine* and *Faustus*,—*Pericles* and *Hamlet*,—*then* let him read the *Jew of Malta*, and he will readily perceive how diligently and earnestly the author must have studied the Shaksperian plays. For the *Jew* differs from its predecessors not only in a freer versification and in a more natural style, but also in several quibbles, and in certain phrases, as, "Who comes here?" "but soft;" two familiar expressions essentially Shaksperian. "Soft" occurs three times in *Endymion* and six times in *Midas*, evidently from the association of ideas; this soft expression was probably a conversational habit with Shakspere, as "noting it down" was a custom with Lyly.

Mr. Dyce justly repudiates the supposition, that Shakspere, from the *Jew of Malta*, "caught anything more than a few trifling hints for the *Merchant of Venice;*" nor is it likely the youthful creator of Aaron would, seven years after, copy from a copy; for Barabas and Ithamore, master and servant, are two unmitigated villains, each having a resemblance to Aaron in *Titus Andronicus;* thus the dying speech of Barabas, in its fiendish malignity, is clearly an imitation of one of Aaron's:—

> *Bar.* "Know, governor, 'twas I that slew thy son,—
> I fram'd the challenge that did make them meet:
> Know, Calymath, I aim'd thy overthrow:
> And had I but escap'd this stratagem,
> I would have brought confusion on you all,
> Damn'd Christian dogs, and Turkish infidels!"—
> *Jew of Malta*, p. 347.

> *Aar.* "Well, let my deeds be witness of my worth.
> I train'd thy brethren to that guileful hole,
> Where the dead corpse of Bassianus lay:
> I wrote the letter that thy father found,
> And hid the gold within the letter mention'd,
> Confederate with the queen and her two sons."
> *Titus Andronicus*, act v., scene 1.

The Jew's love for his daughter is thus ironically described:—

> *Bar.* "I have no charge nor many children,
> But one sole daughter, whom I hold as dear
> As Agamemnon did his Iphigen;
> And all I have is hers;"

he is quite ready to sacrifice her to "raise the wind," and at last poisons her for turning Christian.

But as Aaron, unlike Barabas, has one touch of nature in his composition, so must Ithamore, who, in fact, is Aaron himself, *ita-more*—the Moor again; and so Ithamore falls in love with Bellamira, and addresses to her the following remarkable speech:—

Bell. " I have no husband, sweet, I'll marry thee.
Itha. Content: but we will leave this paltry land,
And sail from hence to Greece, to lovely Greece;—
I'll be thy Jason, thou my golden fleece;—
Where painted carpets o'er the meads are hurl'd,
And Bacchus vineyards overspread the world;
Where woods and forests go in goodly green;—
I'll be Adonis, thou shalt be Love's Queen;
The meads, the orchards, and the prim-rose lanes,
Instead of sedge and reed, bear sugar-canes:
Thou in those groves, by Dis above,
Shalt live with me, and be my love."

The last line is a quotation, slightly varied, from the *Passionate Shepherd to his Love,* a beautiful song of Shakspere's, but most unjustly attributed to Marlowe on the weakest evidence possible. It was originally printed as Shakspere's in the *Passionate Pilgrim,* 1599; but in the following year, 1600, it was published in England's *Helicon,* and subscribed with the name C. Marlowe. So far the one publication neutralises the other; but fifty-three years later, or sixty years after the death of Marlowe, Isaac Walton inserted it "in his *Complete Angler,* under the character of "That smooth song, which was made by Kit Marlowe, now at least fifty years ago; and an *Answer* to it which was made by Sir Walter Raleigh in his younger days." Warburton unhesitatingly gives both to Shakspere; and "snatches of this one are sung by Sir Hugh Evans in the *Merry Wives of Windsor.*" The song of four stanzas, I believe, is Shakspere's, the other two stanzas may be anybody's. Throughout all the acknowledged writings of Marlowe, the nearest approach to this song is the very speech addressed to Bellamira; "we look in vain," says an eminent critic, "for a single familiar image in Marlowe's poetry;" another authority says, "Of an age distinguished for the excellence of its rural poetry, this is, without doubt, the most admirable and finished pastoral." On a dispassionate examination, even granting the *Reply* to have been written by Sir Walter, Marlowe appears to have no more claim to this most admirable and finished pastoral than Barnfield has to Shakspere's *Spenserian Sonnet*.

The last line, then, of Ithamore's speech, "live with me, and be my love," being a quotation from Shakspere's song, carries with it a peculiar significance; and it is very remarkable, whilst *Tamburlaine* and *Faustus* are nearly free

"From jigging veins of rhyming mother-wits,"

this tragedy abounds with rhyming couplets besides this whole speech in rhyme, a speech singularly inappropriate in the mouth of Ithamore, unless a hidden sense be attached to it; there must be some meaning in such an extraordinary revolution in the poet's proceedings; and perhaps Pilia Borza's reply to Bellamira's inquiry about Ithamore, puts us on the right scent, on the true path of discovery:—

Bel. "And where didst meet him?
Pilia. Upon mine own freehold, within forty foot of the gallows, conning his neck-verse, I think it, looking of a friar's execution."

Both Mr. Collier and Mr. Dyce consider, the *Jew of*

Malta was written about 1589 or 1590; it may then be regarded as certain, it was not produced till some time after Nash's *Epistle* prefixed to Greene's *Menaphon.*

We can now readily understand Pilia Borza's observation, that he found Ithamore " within forty foot of the gallows, *conning his neck-verse;*" and when Ithamore says, "I scorn to write a line under a hundred crowns," Pilia significantly replies, "You'd make a rich poet, sir." We can also see the meaning of the journey to Greece, the "by Dis above" being a jocular allusion to his classical ignorance, and the quotation, "live with me and be my love," from Shakspere's pretty song, clearly pointing out the particular individual, to whom these allusions refer. The coincidence about Greece between Marlowe and Lyly in this play and in *Midas*, both written at the same time, confirms the impression, Shakspere must have read the Greek dramatists in their own language, and that William deserved his mama's praise:—

Mrs. Page. "He is a better scholar than I thought he was.
Evans.   He is a good sprag memory."

Furthermore the singular comparison of Barabas' love for his daughter to Agamemnon's love for Iphigenia raises a suspicion, Shakspere may have read up the Greek plays with Marlowe, and, no doubt, paid him handsomely for his services; it also strengthens the opinion, that Ophelia is risen, Phœnix-like, from the ashes of Iphigenia, that Marlowe knew the fact, and that Abigail is his translation of the character, or rather a copy of Ophelia; there is besides much in the bitterness of Barabas, reminding us of Hamlet's causticity to his dear friends the two sponges.

The stertorous breathing, dilated pupil, and insensibility;—the blueness, coldness, and diarrhœa,—are not so distinctive marks of apoplexy and cholera, as the neck-verse, journey to Greece, and "by Dis above," are diagnostic symptoms of the immortal William; consequently "live with me and be my love" must be taken from one of Shakspere's songs; and consequently in this short scene of Satanic comedy, Ithamore stands as his representative, no doubt intended as a compliment, if not a flattering likeness; of course every portrait painter is not a Ross or a Lawrence; so is it equally certain, that Pilia Borza is a self-drawn portrait of the author, a striking likeness and original; not drawn unconsciously, like the self-drawn portraits of Shakspere and Coleridge, but knowingly and intentionally, for is it not said of Parolles, " is it possible, he should know what he is, and be that he is?"

As the *Jew of Malta* appears from the preceding analysis to have been a very studied performance, it must have cost Marlowe much thought and labour, and was probably not produced before the spring of 1590; it was followed by *King John, Edward II.*, and the *Massacre at Paris*, and by the *Taming of a Shrew* in the spring of 1593; *Dido*, as much as belongs to Marlowe, must have been an early work, perhaps written in '88 after the failure of *Dido and Æneas*, and not proceeded with on account of his new engagements with his humourous and satirical patron. We thus see, Marlowe had the tact and wordly wisdom at a great theatrical crisis to stand by "the coming man," and swear himself in as "liegeman to the Dane," and from this time forth he remained the humble follower and close imitator of the mighty dramatist and no less potential manager. We are here reminded of Steele's connexion with Addison, "Addison, says Johnson, never considered Steele as a rival; but Steele lived, as he confesses, under an habitual subjection to the predominating genius of Addison, whom he always mentioned with reverence, and treated with obsequiousness."

During this period of seven years and a half, Marlowe produced nine plays, seven acknowledged to be his, two disputed:—The Two Parts of *Tamburlaine, Faustus, Jew of Malta, King John, Edward II., Massacre at Paris, Taming of a Shrew,* and *Dido;*—whilst Shakspere produced fourteen,—*Two Gentlemen of Verona, Titus Andronicus, All's Well that Ends Well, Dido and Æneas, Hamlet, Love's Labour's Lost, Comedy of Errors, Romeo and Juliet, Henry VI.,* Two Parts of *The Contention, Richard III., Merry Wives of Windsor,* and *Midsummer Night's Dream;*—besides undergoing the fatigues of an actor's life, and the responsibilities of a theatrical manager; and yet not overtasked;—his intellectual powers, like the British oak, steadily increasing, strengthening, and developing themselves; assuredly his was not a life of dissipation, but that of an artist devoted to his profession; truly might he say, "no more like than I to Hercules," but not in Schlegel's sense; for he might have added, a greater than Hercules is here.

Let us now examine Greene's celebrated Address in the *Groatsworth of Wit*;—" Yes, trust them not; for there is an upstart crow beautified with our feathers, that, with his *Tyger's heart wrapt in a player's hyde*, supposes he is as well able to bombast out a blank verse as the best of you, and, being an absolute Johannes-factotum, is in his own conceit the only Shakescene in a country." There cannot be a doubt, Shakspere is alluded to as the upstart crow, and there can be no meaning, no force in the words parodied from a line in the *True Tragedy*,—

" Oh, tyger's heart wrapt in a woman's hide,"

unless that tragedy had been written by Shakspere From the phrase " beautified with our feathers " it can only be inferred, Shakspere had purloined some beautiful passages, some fine sentiments, from the works of Greene and others, and had appropriated them to his own vile purposes; but Greene does not bring forward any direct charge, nor adduce any instances of spoliation; therefore the whole passage may be regarded as a tissue of insinuations and misrepresentations, proceeding from personal animosity and wounded vanity. Besides, the character of the writer should be known, and then the reader may place what trust he pleases on such insinuations unsupported by any evidence :—

" He (Marlowe) had a friend, once *gay and greene*,
  Who died not long before,
  The wofull'st wretch was ever seene,
  The worst e'er woman bore."—*Marlowe*, vol. iii.

That the three plays, *Henry VI.* and the Two Parts of *The Contention*, were really written by Shakspere, and that he did not merely remodel them, rests on the highest authority, on the testimony of a very different character from Greene:—

"And there, though last not least, is Aëtion;
A gentler shepherd may nowhere be found.
Whose Muse full of high thoughts' invention,
Doth like himself heroically sound."—
Colin Clout's Come Home again.

It is incredible Spenser would thus have sung the praises of his friend, had his merits consisted in merely adding some lines and polishing up the works of others, to whom decidedly the praise of "high thoughts' invention" would then have been due.

But that these plays were composed and not merely remodelled by Shakspere, rests on still higher authority, on the word of the poet himself; the concluding lines of the chorus in *Henry V.*, can have no other meaning:—

"and for *their* sake,
In your fair minds let *this* acceptance take."

Where is the force of the plea, unless *Henry VI.* had been written by Shakspere? He could have appealed more directly to the sympathies of the audience on behalf of *Henry V.*, by a reference to the Two Parts of *Henry IV.*; but his real object was to connect *this series* from *Richard II.* to *Henry V.* with the other moiety, thus forming an harmonious whole, one grand historical drama.

But far too much importance has been attached to this passage in the *Groatsworth of Wit*;* it seems to

---

* "With thee I joyne young Juvenal, that byting satyrist, that lastly with me together writ a comedie. Sweet boy, might I advise thee, be advised, and get not many enemies by bitter words."

The critics and commentators have too readily followed Malone's have been merely a temporary outburst of envy and malice; for Greene did not always write thus. In the *Looking-glass for London* Marlowe is satirized as Rasni, King of Nineveh. The following lines in the opening speech of the play identify him with "that atheist Tamburlaine, or blaspheming with the mad priest of the sun":—

> *Ras.* "Great Jewry's God, that foil'd stout Benhadad,
> Could not rebate the strength that Rasni brought;
> For be he God in heaven, yet, viceroys, know,
> Rasni is god on earth, and none but he."

The three Kings attendant on his "royal mightiness" are Shakspere and the two authors of the play, Greene and Lodge. The following lines clearly prove the King of Cilicia to be intended for Shakspere:—

> *K. of Cil.* "Madam, I hope you mean not for to mock me.
> *Alv.* No, king, fair king, my meaning is to yoke thee.
> Hear me but sing of love, then by my sighs,
> My tears, my glancing looks, my changed cheer,
> Thou shalt perceive how I do hold thee dear.
> *K. of Cil.* Your love is fixed on a greater king.
> *Alv.* Tut, women's love it is a fickle thing.
> I love my Rasni for his dignity,
> I love Cilician king for his sweet eye;

---

opinion, that the party here alluded to, is Lodge; but it certainly must be Nash, who was often called Juvenal by the writers of that period. Lodge was not in England at that time; for Greene in the Address prefixed to *Euphues Shadow*, 1592, says,—" one M. Thomas Lodge who nowe is gone to sea with mayster Candish;" besides the *Looking-glass for London* is no comedy, but a religious mystery; and the lines to young Juvenal are written in such a friendly spirit, they might even confirm in an angry man the suspicion of Nash's complicity in the tract.

     I love my Rasni since he rules the world,
     But more I love this kingly little world.
              [Embraces him.
     How sweet he looks! O, were I Cynthia's fere,
     And thou Endymion, I should hold thee dear.
     Thus should mine arms be spread about thy neck,
              [Embraces his neck.
     Thus would I kiss my love at every beck;
              [Kisses him.
     Thus would I sigh to see thee sweetly sleep,
     And if thou waked'st not soon, thus would I weep,
     And thus, and thus, and thus, thus much I love thee.
              [Kisses him.
K. of Cil. For all these vows beshrew me, if I prove ye:
     My faith unto my king shall not be fals'd.
Alv.   Good Lord, how men are coy when they are crav'd!
K. of Cil. Madam, behold our king approacheth nigh.
Alv.   Thou art Endymion, then, no more: heighho, for
     him I die!"
     [Faints while pointing at the King of Cilicia.

Adam, the smith's man, may possibly also be intended for Shakspere; he looks like an imitation of Launce, but awfully addicted to beef and ale:—

 Adam. "Nay, sir, we read in the *Chronicles* that there was a god of our occupation.—Marry, sir, I will stand to it, that a smith in his kind is a physician, a surgeon, and a barber.—I am for you; come, let's away, and yet let me be put in the *Chronicles.*"

His thrashing his master for being jealous may be on the part of Lodge, a sly rap at Greene's jealousy of Shakspere.

The *Looking-glass* appears to have been written in 1591, and in imitation of *Midas;* for Rasni is throughout treated with similar love and reverence; and we seem to have the origin of the play in *Midas,* act fourth, scene fourth, where Eristus and Mellacrites say,—"we will all join and follow Martius," who replies, "My lords, I give you thanks;" and the expression, "Rasni is god on earth," has also its counterpart in *Midas*, when Martius says, "That greediness of Mellacrites, whose heart-strings are made of Plutus' purse-strings, hath made Midas a lump of earth, that should be a god on earth," act two, scene one. As Martius disbelieves the oracles and is portrayed as a contemner of the gods, so Rasni requires the wonders and signs of the anger of God to be explained by natural causes.—If then Rasni be the same individual as Martius, it must be granted, the King of Cilicia is Shakspere.

In the Comical History of *Alphonsus, King of Arragon*, it is within the bounds of probability, that Shakspere is the Hero; Marlowe would be Belinus, King of Naples; and in *Amurack the Great Turk*, lord over so many regions, Greene has beautifully and no less truthfully painted his own discontent and jealousy. When Alphonsus after slaying Flaminius, exclaims:—

> "Go pack thou hence unto the Stygian lake,—
> And if he ask thee who did send thee down,
> Alphonsus say, who now must wear thy crown;"

the audience would immediately remember the grand and fearful scene in the second part of the *Contention*:—

> "Down, down to hell and say I sent thee thither;"*

---

* Who wrote this most Satanic speech? Shakspere, Greene, or Marlowe? Mr. Collier gives it to Greene on account of this passage in Alphonsus; Mr. Dyce to Marlowe on account of the lines:
> "What, will the aspiring blood of Lancaster
> Sink in the ground? I thought it would have mounted."

But may it not rather be held, these resemblances prove, the True and thus Alphonsus, Gloster, and Shakspere would be irrevocably conjoined in their minds.

"Belinus, Fabius, and the Milan Duke, fled for succour to the Turkish court," are Marlowe, Peele, and Nash; the last named is in the *Groatsworth of Wit*, called "Young Juvenal, sweet boy," and in the following lines the three characters are clearly marked:—

> *Alphon.* "Lord, what a pleasure was it to my mind,
> To see Belinus, which not long before
> Did with *his threatenings terrify the gods*,
> Now scud apace from warlike Lælius' blows!
> The Duke of Milan, he increas'd our sport,
> When doubting that his force was over-weak,
> For to withstand, Miles, thy sturdy arm,
> Did give more credence to his frisking skips
> Than to *the sharpness of his cutting blade*.
> What Fabius did to *pleasure* us withal,
> Albinius knows as well as I myself."—
>
> Act iii, scene 1.

Albinius is no doubt Lyly:—

> *Alphon.* "Now to Albinius, which in all my toils
> I have both faithful, yea, and friendly, found."

Alphonsus has also two other warriors on his side, Lælius and Miles; these may be the two other playwrights mentioned in the *Groatsworth of Wit*, of whom Greene says, "let their own work serve to witness against their own wickedness, if they persevere to maintain any more such peasants;" but whoever these two may have been, it is certain Miles and Lælius are very appropriate names for Kyd and Lodge; the little Jeronymo giving

---

Tragedie, or third part of *Henry VI*, was written by Shakspere, and brought out at least several months before either *King Alphonsus* or *Edward the Second*.

Master Nash a good drubbing, and the religious Lodge castigating the irreligious Marlowe. Lodge was not only Greene's friend, but appears to have been warmly attached to Shakspere, and is here named after Lælius, the intimate friend of Scipio Africanus. Peele is probably named Fabius after the great general, who derided Scipio's idea of carrying the war into Africa. Peele is also said to have been jealous of Shakspere. In these names, Fabius and Lælius, Greene evidently intends a most graceful and flattering compliment to Shakspere as Scipio Africanus, the conqueror of Zama.

The invocation of Medea,—Iphigena daughter of Amurack the great Turk,—Faustus his Empress,—and a Faustus, king of Babylon!—what a strange and unmeaning jumble of names, unless they are intended to remind us of Shakspere and Marlowe;—further evidence that the ignorant William had read the Greek dramatists; and again, Amurack encouraging his troops thus significantly speaks :—

> "Besides the same, remember with yourselves
> What foes we have; not mighty Tamburlaine,
> Nor soldiers trained up amongst the wars,
> But fearful boors, pick'd from their rural flock,
> Which, till this time, were wholly ignorant
> What weapons meant, or bloody Mars did crave."—
>
> Act iv.

How applicable are these lines to Shakspere's want of an University education; and by "*fearful boors*" we are reminded of "*such peasants*" as Shakspere, Burbage, & Co.

By the overthrow of Amurack, and the marriage of Alphonsus with Iphigena, and his succession to the empire, Greene acknowledges the superiority of Shakspere as a poet; whether he intended in the Second Part, had such been written, to portray Alphonsus as a beneficent monarch, or as an universal tyrant, may be problematical; but the continuation appeared in a very unexpected form, the hero being a *Johannes-factotum*, and the only Shakescene in the country.

From the examination of these plays it may be inferred, that Greene, like Lyly, took an ardent interest in the early career of Shakspere; but being himself a gifted poet of most varied powers, he could not, without a pang, see the diadem wrested from his brow.

Let us turn back for a few minutes to *Love's Labour's Lost*; it has been shown, that Biron, Armado, and Sir Nathaniel, are Shakspere, Marlowe, and Lyly; the three remaining characters (sonnetteers and poets), Ferdinand, king of Navarre, Longaville, and Dumain, must consequently be Greene, Lodge, and Peele; whilst Moth is a most happy and delightful personation of that "*sweet boy*," Nash; who was called Juvenal, not merely after the Roman satirist, but from his youthful appearance, as in *Pierce Penniless* he speaks of his "beardless years," being then in his twenty-fifth year, and the following lines may have given rise to the name:—

Arm. "How canst thou part sadness and melancholy, my tender juvenal?
Moth. By a familiar demonstration of the working, my tough senior.
Arm. Why tough senior? why tough senior?
Moth. Why tender juvenal? why tender juvenal?
Arm. I spoke it, tender juvenal, &c."—
Act i., scene 2.

We thus see that Shakspere, in the joy of his heart at the success of *Hamlet*, immediately sought to be reconciled with his old friends; and that this comedy, so popular in its own day, and still the universal favourite of youth, was the offspring of his generous feelings, a photographic picture, the sunshine of life, a picnic on a summer's day. As Nash in the *Anatomie of Absurditie*, published in 1589, abuses Greene as the "Homer of women, &c.," it follows, that the celebrated epistle prefixed to *Menaphon* must have appeared in the early part of the year, and have preceded *Love's Labour's Lost*.

It becomes also highly probable, that *Orlando Furioso* was an earlier satire on Marlowe, and that Sacripant, his cunning and formidable foe, was intended for Nash. Nor is it at all improbable, the comedy *lastly* written by Greene and young Juvenal was the continuation of the *Comical History of Alphonsus*, beyond doubt a satirical production and—pity 'tis, 'tis lost.

After this long excursion with Nash, Marlowe, and Greene, it is about time to see after our pleasant Willy, whom we left, if I remember correctly, in a fix, uncertain whether he were Falstaff or Midas. But before proceeding on with the plays, we must first take a look at the sonnets. The joke in the *Merry Wives of Windsor* at Marlowe's expense, "three German devils, three Doctor Faustus's," is very significant.

In the "*Sonnets** *re-arranged*," I have pointed out,

---

* Valuable evidence in support of the opinion, the *Sonnets* were an early production, is the fact, that all the parallel passages in Mr. Staunton's edition, are quoted from the early plays, as *Love's Labour's Lost, Romeo and Juliet, Henry VI.*, and *Merchant of Venice*.

that Marlowe is alluded to in the line, "Was it the proud full sail of his great verse," and that he was also "the better spirit," and that Mephistophiles is the "affable familiar ghost." The probability, that this explanation is the correct one, may be readily seen by reference to the *Tragical History of Dr. Faustus:—*

Faust. "Go, and return to mighty Lucifer,
And meet me in my study at midnight.
Is't not midnight?—come, Mephistophilis,
Veni, veni, Mephistophile!"

[*Enter* LUCIFER, BELZEBUB *and* MEPHISTOPHILIS.]

Luc. "Do so, and we will highly gratify thee. Faustus, we are come from hell to show thee some pastime. Now, Faustus, how dost thou like this?
Faust. Oh, this feeds my soul!
Luc. Tut, Faustus! in hell is all manner of delight.
Faust. Oh, might I see hell, and return again. How happy were I then!
Luc. Thou shalt; I will send for thee at midnight.
C. of Lor. My lord, it may be some ghost, newly crept out of Purgatory, come to beg a pardon of your Holiness.
Pope. It may be so.—Friars, prepare a dirge to lay the fury of this ghost.
Emp. They say thou hast a familiar spirit, by whom thou canst accomplish what thou list."

It therefore appears that ten sonnets, forming together one epistle, are written in good-humoured ridicule of Marlowe, as Tamburlaine and Faustus, the two nicknames by which he was generally known. "Oh, how I faint," like a sentimental young lady in hysterics, is either a quizzical expression or else a very weak one, worthy of the Hamlet of Goethe and Coleridge. But the critics and commentators have taken a very different view of these sonnets. Thus writes Mr. Boaden:—

"The *Sonnets* not only allude distinctly to Daniel (as the *better spirit*), but very critically point out some other retainers of the Pembroke family. The poet hardly preserves his temper when describing the combination against him:

> "Was it *his* spirit, by *spirits taught to write
> Above a mortal pitch*, that struck me dead?
> No! neither *he*, nor his compeers, by night
> Giving him aid, my verse astonished.
> He, nor that affable *familiar ghost*,
> Which *nightly* gulls him with intelligence,
> As victors, of my silence cannot boast."

"Alluding, perhaps," says Mr. Stevens, "to the celebrated Dr. Dee's pretended intercourse with an angel and other familiar spirits." There can be no doubt about it—the fact is upon record. Queen Elizabeth and the Pembroke family were Dee's chief patrons. Their exalted minds and various accomplishments did not exempt them from the mania of their times, though the sounder philosophy of Shakspere led him thus to denounce the Charlatans, who then infested the great, and upon fantastical science grounded predictions, which hung like a mildew upon a long existence.—*On the Sonnets of Shakspere.*

And this is the sort of erudite and illogical stuff that persuaded Hallam, and nearly all the intellects of Britain—even Rab himself, that sagacious Scotch dog— to believe that the healthy, jocular, and satirical Shakspere wrote, in his thirty-fifth year, maudlin sentimentality to a profligate young nobleman in his nineteenth year.

I have pointed out in the Introduction to the "*Sonnets re-arranged*," that Shakspere became acquainted with the Earl of Southampton in 1589, and for several years watched over him like a guardian; that in October, 1591, he addressed to him a comic-heroic poem, and that the couplets, promising immortality to his friend, are merely a cheerful refrain to prevent the poem degenerating into a monotonous and adulatory strain. I have also shown, they were collected together by William Herbert, Earl of Pembroke, and given to Thomas Thorpe for publication.

Although there are several editions of *Shakspere's Poems*, yet it is to the *Sonnets*, I imagine, they owe their principal attraction, since the *Venus and Adonis* abounds rather too freely with lascivious descriptions, and the *Lucrece* is such a "crabbed and quaint production," it is no easy matter to work through it; whilst the *Sonnets* in richness of imagery and mellifluous versification rival the *Venus and Adonis* without its indelicacy; and, full of tenderness and noble thoughts, they abound in the moral and poetical beauties of the *Lucrece*, without its dryness; I therefore ventured to lay before the public a new edition of the *Sonnets*, arranged on a plan never yet attempted, and apparently never thought of, viz:—to select and re-arrange (not to re-divide, but to re-sort) the little poems, which are evidently addressed to his friend; and which, thus re-arranged, form a clear and connected history; further, from the first '126' are ejected those, which are addressed to a female; by this simple process the *Sonnets* have been removed from cloud-land, and restored to the domain of healthy literature, making a very pleasant and readable book, highly interesting and autobiographical.

But the most interesting feature in the *Sonnets* is the evidence, that Shakspere had formed a very close intimacy with a dark-haired lady, apparently of about twelve months' duration, from the summer of 1592, to the summer of 1593, and which then came to an abrupt end by the amorous tigress transferring her caresses to his friend, the young Earl of Southampton. She must have been an Italian, of some rank, the wife of one of the merchant princes of Venice at least, or the Ambassadress herself, if not the wife of an English nobleman. That she was an Italian may be inferred from the fact, that in all his plays after this period, Shakspere shows such an intimate acquaintance with the manners and customs of Italy, as to have given rise to the supposition, he had visited Italy; but in truth his Italy was a lady with raven-black eyes. Now it is very remarkable, there are three dark ladies in the plays, Hermia, Katharine, and Cleopatra, three black witches, equally ready with their fists, like the lady in the *Sonnets*, who had decidedly a will of her own; that she stood as the original of the other three cannot be doubted.

This lady, with her black and mourning eyes and a will of her own, reminds us of Byron's two Venetian loves;—Marianna, with "the large black oriental eyes with that peculiar expression in them, which is seen rarely among Europeans;"—Margarita, "very fine black eyes, a thorough Venetian, with all their naiveté and pantaloon humour, and a devilish spirit of some sort within her." The duration of Shakspeare's actual enchantment reminds us, that the wisest of the Greeks, Ulysses, remained a whole year under the Circèan spell.

As the *Midsummer Night's Dream* and the *Merry Wives of Windsor* were both written about the same time and under similar circumstances, they should be examined and compared together with reference to the passages, which may be considered, rightly or wrongly, applicable to Shakspere.

The following lines in the *Midsummer Night's Dream* have frequently been adduced as evidence, that the poet had made an unfortunate marriage :—

Lys.	"Ah me! for aught that ever I could read, Could ever hear by tale or history, The course of true love never did run smooth: But, either it was different in blood ;—
Her.	O cross! too high to be enthrall'd to low!
Lys.	Or else misgraffed, in respect of years ;—
Her.	O spite! too old to be engag'd to young!
Lys.	Or else it stood upon the choice of friends ;—
Her.	O hell; to choose love by another's eye!
Lys.	Or, if there were a sympathy in choice, War, death, or sickness did lay siege to it."—

Act i. scene 1.

How do these lines affect Shakspere? they are merely the usual complaint of lovers contraried by their parents; "misgraffed in respect of years" is the only unfavorable expression, all the rest actually confirm the supposition of his domestic happiness; for it is universally granted, he married for love, and apparently without asking permission either of friends or parents. These lines then, though so often quoted, are no proof Shakspere lived unhappily with his wife; nor is there any evidence or tradition, that she ever lost his affection; though for a time he laboured under a delusion, under the fascination of an extraordinary woman. The story of his domestic infelicity was first started something more than a century ago, by Oldys misinterpreting one of the *Sonnets*.

Another passage in this comedy is supposed to contain an allusion to Greene:—

Lys. [*reads*] "The battle with the Centaurs' to be sung
By an Athenian eunuch to the harp.
The. We'll none of that: that have I told my love,
In glory of my kinsman Hercules.
Lys. The riot of the tipsy Bacchanals
Tearing the Thracian singer in their rage.
The. That is an old device, and it was play'd
When I from Thebes came last a conqueror.
Lys. The thrice three Muses mourning for the death
Of learning, late deceas'd in beggary.
The. That is some satire, keen, and critical,
Not sorting with a nuptial ceremony."—Act v., scene 1.

The "learning late deceas'd in beggary," Mr. C. Knight observes, refers to the death of the poet Greene, and "some satire keen and critical," to the famous controversy of Nash and Gabriel Harvey. But let us follow up the scent, trace the fox to his hole. and unearth him;—surely the Thracian singer can be no other than Shakspere himself; and how appositely does Mr. Ignorance speak through Theseus, "it's an old story, played after my return from Thebes as conqueror,"—*after Hamlet;* —and the Athenian eunuch must be Chettle, the editor, who omitted some offensive passages in Greene's *Groatsworth of Wit.*

Furthermore, can there be any reasonable doubt, that the beautiful lines on "the imperial votaress in maiden meditation fancy-free" were written after the *Merry Wives of Windsor,* and are Endymion's thanks for Cynthia's kiss?

It must then be confessed, there are in this *Dream* three passages of a decidedly personal nature; and those critics, who consider the first, as proof of his unhappy marriage, must for the sake of consistency, acknowledge, Hermia is the lady of the *Sonnets;* and who is Lysander? like Valentine, he is "a gentleman and well deriv'd;" his friend Demetrius is certainly Marlowe. Demetrius comes upon us at first as a swaggerer, is spoken of as a coward, and is the only character that uses high-flown language; the lines addressed to Helen, are essentially Marlovian:

"The one I'll slay, the other slayeth me.
Thou told'st me, they were stol'n into this wood,
And here am I, and wood (wild) within this wood."
"Yet, you, the murderer, look as bright, as clear,
As yonder Venus in her glimmering sphere."
"O Helen, goddess, nymph, perfect, divine!
To what, my love, shall I compare thine eyne!
Crystal is muddy. O, how ripe in show
Thy lips, those kissing cherries, tempting grow!
That pure congealed white, high Taurus snow,
Fann'd with the eastern wind, turns to a crow,

>   When thou hold'st up thy hand; O let me kiss
>   This princess of pure white, this seal of bliss!"
> *Puck.* "Thou coward, art thou bragging to the stars,
>   Telling the bushes that thou look'st for wars,
>   And will not come? Come, recreant; come, thou child;
>   I'll whip thee with a rod; he is defil'd
>   That draws a sword on thee!
>   Ho, ho! ho, ho! Coward why com'st thou not?"

To Lysander Puck merely calls out:—

> "Here villain; drawn and ready. Where art thou?"

But say the critics, Demetrius is a punster, and Marlowe was a learned man, with no wit or humour in him. "Soft you now," softly there, my friends! in *Tamburlaine* and *Faustus* there is not a single pun or quibble, except some few amongst the clowns, probably borrowed from the common stock of clownage; but in the *Jew of Malta* a change comes o'er the scene, and to the great amusement of Shakspere and Lyly, Marlowe, by friction with such sharp blades, becomes a wit, and so Demetrius puns:—

> "Haply some hapless man hath conscience."
> "Give me a ream of paper; we'll have a kingdom
>   Of gold for't."—*The Jew of Malta.*

realm was frequently written ream, says Mr. Dyce. Other quibbles may be found, and particularly in *Edward II.*

There is also in this Dream an allusion to Lyly, at least a reminiscence of him; Bottom says, "I see their knavery; this is to make an ass of me;" he then sings a song evidently a paraphrase of the bird-song in *Campaspe*, ending with the note of the cuckoo. And who can say, sweet bully Bottom with his ass's head is not a burlesque of the poet himself, as *Midas*; 'tis evident

Shakspere delighted in the joke, and roars over it like a sucking-dove, an 'twere any nightingale; besides, Bottom "is as well able to bombast out a blank-verse as the best of you, and being an absolute Johannes-fac-totum, is in his own conceit the only Shakescene in the *play*;" and when Bottom says,—"my chief humour is for a tyrant: I could play Ercles rarely;—This is Ercles' vein, a tyrant's vein,"—is it not an allusion to the *Groatsworth of Wit*, where the player recounts to Roberto how he had "terribly thundered" the *Twelve Labours of Hercules*.

Do we not then see in "the jealous Oberon" a divine translation of Greene, the poet's forgiveness in the apotheosis of his early friend, and the Blackfriars Company in :—

> "A crew of patches, rude mechanicals,
> That work for bread upon Athenian stalls,
> Were met together to rehearse a play,
> Intended for great Theseus' nuptial day,
> The shallowest thick-skin of that barren sort,
> Who Pyramus presented in their sport,
> Forsook his scene and enter'd in a brake:
> When I did him at this advantage take,
> An ass's nowl I fixed on his head,
> When in that moment [so it came to pass]
> Titania wak'd, and straightway lov'd an ass."

As Titania is another name for Diana or Cynthia, may not the last line refer to the high favour Shakspere was in at court at that time.

Do we not also see in Puck the poet's forgiveness of Nash; has not Nash repented, has he not humbly sued for pardon :—

> "Without redresse complaynes my carelesse verse,
> And Midas ears relent not at my moane;"

and did he not at Christmas indignantly call the *Groatsworth of Wit* " a scald, trivial, lying pamphlet," and shall not Valentine forgive:—

> "Who by repentance is not satisfied,
> Is nor of heaven nor earth."

and really Nash appears to be very appositely represented by Puck, "that shrewd and knavish sprite;" for there seems more a love of mischief than maliciousness in his remarks against his friends in the epistle prefixed to *Astrophel;* and it should not be overlooked, Puck here holds the same relative position to Oberon, as Dello to Motto, and Nash to Greene.

That Greene and Nash are aimed at in Oberon and Puck cannot be doubted; it is made certain by the fact, that the comedy was written soon after the publication of Greene's tract, and Shakspere replies to his unjust charges through Titania:—

> *Tita.* "These are the forgeries of jealousy;
> And never, since the middle summer's spring,
> Met we on hill, in dale—
> But with thy brawls thou hast disturbd our sport."

It has been suggested, this comedy was composed as an allegorical pageant in celebration of some nobleman's marriage; be that as it may, 'tis certain,—Theseus and Hippolyta dance attendance on *the squabbles of a set of strolling vagabonds;*—such is the raw material, out of which the enchanter has weaved this finest of gossamer webs.

As allusion has already been made to the fair vestal

throned by the west, it is now time to take a peep at the *Vision of Oberon*.—

Obe. "My gentle Puck, come hither. Thou rememberest,
Since once I sat upon a promontory,
And heard a mermaid, on a dolphin's back,
Uttering such dulcet, and harmonious breath,
That the rude sea grew civil at her song;
And certain stars shot madly from their spheres,
To hear the sea-maid's music.
Puck. I remember.
Obe. That very time I saw—but thou couldst not—
Flying between the cold moon and the earth,
Cupid all-armed; a certain aim he took
At a fair Vestal, throned by the West,
And loosed a love-shaft smartly from his bow,
As it should pierce a hundred thousand hearts;
But I might see young Cupid's fiery shaft
Quench'd in the chaste beams of the wat'ry moon,
And the Imperial Votaress passed on,
In maiden-meditation, fancy-free.
Yet mark'd I where the bolt of Cupid fell:
It fell upon a little western flower,—
Before, milk-white; now purple with Love's wound,—
And maidens call it Love-in-idleness."

According to Warburton, the mermaid is Mary, Queen of Scots; by the dolphin is denoted her marriage with the Dauphin of France; and by "certain stars" are meant certain English nobles, who fell in her quarrel.

According to Mr. Boaden the first part of the *Vision* refers to the pageantry at Kenilworth, where there was a mermaid, also a dolphin with a band of music in its stomach, but not with a mermaid on its back, and the stars are the fireworks; and he considers the little western flower to be Amy Robsart; but the Reverend Mr.

Halpin, though agreeing with Boaden as to the mermaid, the dolphin, and stars, considers the little flower to be the Countess of Essex, and further, that Cupid is the Earl of Leicester, the moon, Queen Elizabeth, and the earth, the Countess of Sheffield;—he also gives a similar interpretation to Lyly's comedy of *Endymion*. All the commentators appear to be divided between these three interpretations, with variations; Mr. Hunter considers Cupid's shaft as aimed at the Duke of Anjou.

But if Warburton's explanation is now generally rejected, as being highly offensive to Queen Elizabeth, and no less so to the memory of the poet; the other solution is only less objectionable, because it is less offensive.

On examining this celebrated passage we find it divided into two parts, into two allegories, totally distinct, connected only by time; and that, whilst the second image is purely classical, the first is Elizabethan, that is according to the pageants of those days, and must have been " perfectly intelligible to contemporary ears." As the poet's intention is to offer a compliment, a poetical tribute to the Queen, perhaps for some gracious favour received, all the allusions and images would be of a pleasing nature, gratifying to the feelings of his royal Mistress; he would never dream of presenting to her the ghastly head of Queen Mary, nor the heads of her rebellious nobles, nor the bleeding heart of an Amy Robsart; all the allusions must be readily comprehended, and agreeable to a London audience, neither play nor allegory having been written to puzzle the brains of the learned; as the pleasures of Kenilworth had occurred more than seventeen years ago, they must have been forgotten, if ever known to the Londoners; and though the visit of the Duke of Anjou occurred only eleven years ago, and must have been well remembered by a London audience, yet it was highly distasteful to the nation; consequently Cupid's shaft can refer neither to the Duke of Anjou nor to the Earl of Leicester. How then is the allegory to be explained? who is the mermaid? evidently no common being, she rules the waves, and stars shoot from their spheres to listen to her song. Perhaps as there is a sort of free-masonry in the poetical academe, Byron can assist us: in the *Hall of Arimanes* the spirits thus hymn forth;—

" in his hand
The sceptre of the elements, which tear
Themselves to chaos at his high command!
He breatheth—and a tempest shakes the sea;"

but at the dulcet and harmonious breath of the seamaid, of the *Virgin Queen*, "the rude sea grew civil;" and "certain stars shot madly from their spheres" can only mean the suitors of the beautiful young Queen, "mad for thy love," Elizabeth.*

Oberon, seated on a promontory, sees on a dolphin's back a mermaid, the mistress of the sea, the waves obedient to her high command,—an image not very unintelligible to modern Britons, and perhaps some can remember seeing:—

" Flying between the cold moon and the earth,
Cupid all-arm'd; a certain aim he took

---

* " She was a lady of great beauty, of decent stature, and of an excellent shape. In her youth she was adorned with a more than usual maiden modesty; her skin was of pure white, and her hair of a yellow colour, her eyes were beautiful and lively."—*Bohun's Character of Queen Elizabeth.*

> At a fair Vestal, throned by the West,
> And loosed a love-shaft smartly from his bow,
> As it should pierce a hundred thousand hearts;
> And deep into the maiden's heart it pierc'd,
> But Hymen heal'd the wound; and from the blood
> That fell, sprang many a sweet and lovely flower,
> A German Lily, and an English Rose,
> The expectancy and rose of the fair state."

Thus the mermaid is Queen Elizabeth seated on her throne, seated in the affections of her people, and England is the dolphin; consequently, these beautiful lines form two Io Pæans to the praise and glory of Cynthia, recalling to her mind the happy days of the first year of her reign.

But what does Oberon mean by saying:—

> "That very time I saw—but thou could'st not;"

Does he not class Puck *on a level with himself,* when he says:—

> "But we are spirits of another sort:
> I with the morning's love have oft made sport;"—
> Act iii., scene 2.

Oho! do you mark that? a rat, dead for a ducat, dead!

> "We won't go home 'till morning,
> Till daylight doth appear;"—
> *Hymn to Bacchus.*

Nash was born in 1567, and Greene must have been in 1558, at least five or six years old;—therefore Puck could not, but Oberon did see the first year of the Queen's reign;—after this, it must be granted, Oberon and Puck are Greene and Nash, and that Shakspere knows how to forgive.

It is perhaps scarcely necessary to mention, that

Shakspere constantly gives a pleasing signification to the word *mermaid*, using it synonymously with *siren*, which is still retained in a complimentary sense, though the other has disappeared with the pageants:—

Ant. S. " O, train me not, sweet mermaid, with thy note,
　　　　　To drown me in thy sister's flood of tears;
　　　　　Sing, siren, for thyself, and I will dote:
　　　　　　Spread o'er the silver waves thy golden hairs,
　　　　　　And as a bride* I'll take thee and there lie."—
　　　　　　　　Comedy of Errors, act iii., scene 2.

Eno. " Her gentlewomen, like the Nereides,
　　　　So many *seamaids*,† tended her i' the eyes,
　　　　And made their bends adornings: at the helm
　　　　A seeming Mermaid steers."—
　　　　　　Antony and Cleopatra, act ii., scene 2.

As the *Midsummer-Night's Dream* and Marlowe's *Taming of a Shrew* were written at the same time and

---

* The beauty and appropriateness of this image cannot be fully understood unless the reader is aware, that " brides formerly walked to church with their hair hanging loose behind. Anne Bullen's was thus dishevelled, when she went to the altar with King Henry VIII.;" and at the marriage of the Princess Elizabeth with the Palsgrave, "the bride came into the chapel with a coronet of pearl on her head, and her hair dishevelled and hanging down over her shoulders." As Mr. Staunton says, "for *bride* I am responsible," we presume it is another of his happy suggestions.

† The usual reading, *mermaids*, is evidently a misprint, probably caused by the eye confusing *seamaids* with the *seeming mermaid* underneath. The Nereides were not mermaids in the strict sense; "they are commonly represented as young and handsome virgins;"—"in works of art as youthful and beautiful maidens;"—but "sometimes as half woman and half fish;"—Thetis, the mother of Achilles, it may be presumed, was not one of the latter class. These lines may be regarded as further evidence of Shakspere's thorough knowledge of classical mythology.—" *Tended her i' the eyes*," that is, about her person; had Antony and Warburton been her handmaids, they would, no doubt, have made their bends *adorings*.

on the same subject, a vixen and a shrew; however erroneous the opinion may be regarded, it is possible the origin of both was some trivial misunderstanding at a pic-nic, when the lady exhibited unequivocal signs of a shrewish disposition; and the two poets afterwards agreed each to write a comedy on the occasion:—

> " And in the wood, a league without the town,
> Where I did meet thee once with Helena
> To do observance to a morn of May,
> There will I stay for thee."

As the interlude of Pyramus and Thisbe in the *Midsummer-Night's Dream* is a travestie of *Romeo and Juliet,* there must be some link, some intimate connexion between the comedy and tragedy; and it is highly probable, a natural supposition, that Shakspere, in the earlier stages of their acquaintance, with his dramatic eye saw through the heart of the Italian lady, and painted her as Juliet, the child of instinct and passion. And as the first part of *Henry VI.* was written about the same period, it follows, as a reasonable inference, this lady stood for Margaret of Anjou; the words are very remarkable:—

Mar. " Wilt thou accept of ransom, yea or no?
Suf.   Fond man! remember that thou hast a wife;
         Then how can Margaret be thy paramour.   [*aside.*
Mar.   I were best to leave him, for he will not hear.
Suf.   There all is marr'd; there lies a cooling card.
Mar.   He talks at random; sure the man is mad.
Suf.   And yet a dispensation may be had.

Mar.   And yet I would that you would answer me.
Suf.   I'll win this lady Margaret.   For whom?
         Why, for my king: Tush! that's a wooden thing.
Mar.   He talks of wood; it is some carpenter."

The Lady then plays the *asides* in her turn, thereby showing she has something of the "infinite variety" of Cleopatra:—

Suf.   " Lady, wherefore talk you so?
Mar.   I cry you mercy, 'tis but *quid* for *quo*."
First Part of Henry VI., act v., scene 3.

We thus see, the lady of the *Sonnets* is the type of so many female characters; the wool, out of which were spun so many yarns, Juliet, Hermia, Katharine, Margaret of Anjou, and Cleopatra, all evidently sisters, daughters of one mother. And we also see how Shakspere, forgetting his butterfly character, thoughtlessly, like a moth hovering around the flame of a candle, singes his wings and falls—a victim to high art, the looking too curiously into one female heart.

To this list must be added Rosaline in *Love's Labour's Lost*, since Biron's description of his love is almost a transcript from the *Sonnets;* and the following passage proves that the twenty-first Sonnet, edition 1609, was addressed to a lady, and was not a piece of silly sentimentalism addressed to a young nobleman:—

Biron.   "Lend me the flourish of all gentle tongues,—
           Fye, painted rhetoric! O, she needs it not.
           To things of sale a seller's praise belongs;
             She passes praise."—
Love's Labour's Lost, act iv., scene 3.

"Let them say more that like of hear-say well;
I will not praise, that purpose not to sell."—
Sonnet 106, ed. 1859.

It may then be conjectured, Shakspere was presented to this Italian lady early in 1589, as the successful playwright of *Hamlet;* that during the next three years he had, on several occasions as author or manager, the honour of a few gracious words from her ladyship; but she unfortunately, on recognizing herself as *Juliet*, appropriated or misapplied to herself the passionate utterances of *Romeo;* and, yielding her heart to the soft delusion, began taking a warmer interest in the author; although he, on his side, had been merely dramatizing his poetical imaginings; and if in *Henry VI.* Shakspere is really speaking through Suffolk, there cannot be a doubt, though Suffolk be violently smitten, the poet's heart remains untouched. Mr. Lewis, in his *Life of Goethe*, speaking of the image of Friderika being banished by Charlotte Buff, says, "It was an imaginative passion, in which the poet was more implicated than the man. Lotte excited his imagination, the romance of his position heightened the charm by giving an unconscious security to his feelings;" she was betrothed to Kestner. How much more forcibly do these remarks apply to Shakspere, speaking through Suffolk:—

"Fond man! remember that thou hast a wife;"

and especially when Suffolk at the royal conference further observes:—

Suf. "Marriage is a matter of more worth,
Than to be dealt in by attorneyship;
Not whom he will, but whom his grace affects,
Must be companion of his nuptial bed:
And therefore, lords, since he affects her most,

> It most of all these reasons bindeth us,
> In our opinions she should be preferr'd.
> For what is wedlock forced, but a hell,
> An age of discord and continual strife?
> Whereas the contrary bringeth forth bliss,
> And is a pattern of celestial peace."—
>
> *Henry VI.*, act v., scene 5.

It is a singular circumstance, that whilst the pestilence was desolating England in 1592 and '93, the moral plague was also, hawk-like, tiring on the soul of the noblest of her sons. It is also singular, that whilst in 1588 all the bravest hearts in England, though resolute to do their duty, must have felt anxious about the coming contest, Shakspere also was oppressed with anxiety, but energetically trained himself for his contest, the crisis of his poetical career; and England and her spiritual incarnation were each triumphant in the destruction of the *Armada* and the success of *Hamlet*. But it is, perhaps, still more singular, that Shakspere in his twenty-ninth year should have written the *Venus and Adonis* as a moral epistle; the intention was good, though the means were bad; and Providence, it seems, treated him accordingly, meting out to him a reward and punishment in accordance with his matter and his meaning; he lost, though sore was the trial, his plague, his fancy-love; but was rewarded by a return to a healthy state of his moral and religious nature. Just one hundred and ten years after, a similar obliquity of vision occurred in another intellectual giant, when Swift wrote a *Tale of a Tub*, of which it is said, "there cannot be a doubt, that Swift thought this performance calculated to serve the Church of England." That the

Venus and Adonis was written at this period, and for a special purpose, may be surmised from the alteration of the catastrophe, since Stevens remarks, the common and more pleasing fable assures us :—

"When bright Venus yielded up her charms,
The blest Adonis languish'd in her arms."

Shakspere's history during the next six months, the summer and autumn of 1593, is most legibly told in the *Sonnets*. It is evident from the following extracts, *vide Sonnets re-arranged*, the poet's conscience has awakened to the errors of his own conduct, although he still believes in the innocence of his friend; whose morals, however, have already been sapped by the corrupt society of Marlowe, and by the glowing stanzas of the *Venus and Adonis* :—

"With mine own weakness being best acquainted,
  Upon thy part I can set down a story
Of faults conceal'd, wherein I am attainted,
  That thou, in losing me, shall win much glory."—
Sonnet 66.

"Ah! do not, when my heart hath 'scaped this sorrow
  Come in the rearward of a conquer'd woe."—
Sonnet 68.

"Ah! wherefore with infection should he live,
  And with his presence grace impiety."—
Sonnet 72.

And in the 86th he earnestly appeals to his friend, now become a *roué* and sowing his wild oats, to reform and sin no more :—

"But do not so; I love thee in such sort,
  As thou being mine, mine is thy good report."

In the autumn of this year, 1593, Shakspere wrote *Edward III.* The allusion to Lucretia appears to be positive evidence, the play must have been written before his own poem, and perhaps suggested to him the idea of dedicating the Lucrece to the Earl of Southampton; and thus fulfilling, in a very unexpected manner, his "Vow to take advantage of all idle hours, till I have honoured you with some graver labour." This play contains a quotation from one of the *Sonnets* :—

"Lilies that fester smell far worse than weeds;"

and the following line,

"I might perceive his eye in her eye lost,
His ear to drink her sweet tongue's utterance,"

is identical with,

"My ears have not yet drunk a hundred words
Of that tongue's uttering."—
Romeo and Juliet, act ii.

We thus find, *Edward III.* fastens himself to Shakspere by three strong hooks, besides the unanimous opinion of the German critics, corroborated by the words of an eminent English critic, "We look in vain for some known writer of the period, whose works exhibit a similar combination of excellences."

This play is an example of Shakspere's wonderful art in selecting, since it was written with a two-fold object; the first part was personal, according to the immemorial custom of poets, who find relief by giving vent to their feelings in verse, for

"Orpheus' harp was strung with poets' sinews;"

and the second part was written to rouse the martial

ardour of the nation, which was then rather languid; the Commons did not like the taxes in 1593. This is some evidence that Shakspere was a loyal subject, and did not regard " good Queen Bess" as "*a tyrant,*" according to the lamentable explanation of the *Sonnet* 107, ed. 1609; " the great popularity she enjoyed proves, that she did not infringe any *established* liberties of the people;" that he, " who did so take Eliza," should instantly, the breath scarcely out of her body, so insult her memory, is incredible; " the mortal moon hath her eclipse endured," is a genuine Shaksperian expression; she lives but a month, and is therefore excessively mortal, though not a " human mortal;" has not such " a celerity in dying" as Cleopatra; the line should be compared with a passage in *Hamlet* :—

Hor.   " and the moist star,
  Upon whose influence Neptune's empire stands,
  Was sick almost to dooms-day with eclipse."—
           Act i., scene 1.

This play, *Edward III*, is divided into two parts;— " In the first part the point of the action turns upon the love of the king for the beautiful Countess of Salisbury, whom he had released from the besieging Scottish army. The whole of this connexion is no further mentioned in the following part; it comes to a total conclusion at the end of the second act, where the king, conquered, and at the same time strengthened, by the virtuous greatness of the countess, renounces his passion, and becomes again the master of himself. The countess then disappears wholly from the scene, which is changed to the victorious campaign of Edward III, and his heroic son

the Black Prince. The play thus falls into two different parts,—In the first two acts we have the Edward of romance, a puling lover, a heartless seducer, a despot, and then a penitent. In the three last acts we have the Edward of history,—the ambitious hero, the stern conqueror, the affectionate husband, the confiding father."
—*Pictorial Shakspere.*

How applicable is this to Shakspere from the autumn of 1592 to the autumn of 1594; only instead of being the heartless seducer, he was himself most probably the one led astray, as he says in defence of his friend:—

"And when a woman woos, what woman's son
Will sourly leave her 'till she have prevail'd."

"There is a very long and somewhat ambitious scene, in which the king instructs his secretary to describe his passion in verse. During the tempest of Edward's passion, the Prince of Wales arrives at the Castle of Roxburgh, and the conflict in the mind of the king is well imagined:—

Edw. "I see the boy. O, how his mother's face,
Moulded in his, corrects my stray'd desire,
And rates my heart, and chides my thievish eye;
Who, being rich enough in seeing her,
Yet seeks elsewhere: and basest theft is that
Which cannot check itself on poverty.—
Now, boy, what news?
Prince. I have assembled, my dear lord and father,
The choicest buds of all our English blood,
For our affairs in France; and here we come,
To take direction from your majesty.
Edw. Still do I see in him delineate
His mother's visage; those his eyes are hers,

>   Who, looking wistly on me, make me blush;
>   For faults against themselves give evidence:
>   Lust is a fire; and men, like lanthorns, show
>   Light lust within themselves, even through themselves.
>   Away, loose silks of wavering vanity!
>   Shall the large limit of fair Brittany
>   By me be overthrown? and shall I not
>   Master this little mansion of myself?
>   Give me an armour of eternal steel;
>   I go to conquer kings; and shall I then
>   Subdue myself, and be my enemy's friend?
>   It must not be.—Come, boy, forward, advance!
>   Let's with our colours sweep the air of France.
> Lod.   My liege, the countess with a smiling cheer,
>   Desires access unto your majesty.
>   *Advancing from the door and whispering him.*
> Edw.   Why, there it goes! that very smile of hers
>   Hath ransom'd captive France; and set the king,
>   The dauphin, and the peers, at liberty.—
>   Go, leave me, Ned, and revel with thy friends."

"The countess enters, and with the following scene suddenly terminates the ill-starr'd passion of the king;

> Edw.   "&c., &c.
>   I am awaked from this idle dream."

"The remarks of Ulrici upon this portion of the play are conceived upon his usual principle of connecting the action and characterisation of Shakspere's dramas with the development of a high moral, or rather Christian principle.—The concluding observation of Ulrici is—'Truly, if this piece, as the English critics assert, is not Shakspere's own, it is a shame for them that they have done nothing to recover from forgetfulness the name of this second Shakspere, this twin-brother of their great poet.'—'There is one thing wanting,' says Mr. Knight, 'to make the writer a twin-brother,' which is found in *all* those productions, [historical plays;] Where is the *comedy* of Edward III?" If the reader should be of opinion, that in these interesting extracts Shakspere is giving utterance to his own thoughts and feelings, he can readily answer the suggestive query, "Where is the *comedy* of Edward III.?"

Having thus "awaked from this idle dream" the poet fights the good fight again in Lucrece, published in May, 1594; an effective counterblast to the *Venus and Adonis*. In the same year in a more softened mood, though still haunted by the image of the *Ethiop* he composes the *Merchant of Venice*, his mind now dwelling on that " gentle spirit."

> "Whose sunny locks
> Hang on her temples like a golden fleece;"

In fact we here behold a scene in real life the reverse of Faustus with his good and evil angel:—

G. Ang. "Sweet Faustus, leave that execrable art.
Faust. Contrition, prayer, repentance,—what of them?
G. Ang. Oh, they are means to bring thee unto heaven!
E. Ang. Rather illusions, fruits of lunacy,
 That make men foolish that do trust them most.
G. Ang. Sweet Faustus, think of heaven and heavenly things."

However distinct the characters may be, Jessica is evidently intended for Juliet's sister; she has'nt a thought for her father:—

"I will make fast the doors, and gild myself
With some more ducats and be with you straight."

Mr. Hunter in his *Illustrations* observes, "We may remark, however, upon this part of the scene, that it exhibits a curious proof, that when Shakspere delineated, in a manner to make the scene visible to every eye, the garden of Portia, he thought of the garden he had himself created of the Capulets at Verona. The passages which open a view of this little process of the poet's mind are these: *Portia.*—"Swear by your double self;" *Juliet.*—"Swear by your gracious self." *Bassanio.*—"The blessed candles of the night;" *Romeo.*—"Night's candles are burnt out." Bassanio's hyperbolical compliment to the eyes of Portia,—

"We should hold day with the Antipodes
If you should walk in absence of the sun,"

is not more worthy of the poet than the words which he had put into the mouth of Romeo,—

"Her eye in heaven
Would through the airy regions stream so bright
That birds would sing and think it were not night."

Nor can we avoid the supposition, that in the garden scene Shakspere is speaking through Lorenzo, and discoursing most sweetly "of heaven and heavenly things" in the character of tutor or instructor to his companion; and considering the time and circumstances under which this play was composed, the following passage is peculiarly significant:—

Lor. "And now, good sweet, say thy opinion,
How dost thou like the lord Bassanio's wife.

Jes. Past all expressing: it is very meet,
  The lord Bassanio live an upright life;
  For, having such a blessing in his lady,
  He finds the joys of heaven here on earth.—
Act iii., scene 5.

And how pleasing it is to believe, the following lines were intended for his dearest friend, John Lyly:—

Bass. "The dearest friend to me, the kindest man,
  The best condition'd and unwearied spirit
  In doing courtesies; and one in whom
  The ancient Roman honour more appears,
  Than any that draws breath in Italy."—
Act iii., scene 2.

In 1596, having gained a thorough conquest over himself, not a trace of the disease remaining, Shakspere writes a satirical farewell to the lady of the *Sonnets* in the *Taming of the Shrew*:—

  "For patience she will prove a second Grissell,
  And Roman Lucrece for her chastity."

Grumio's speech fixes the date and shows, that Petruchio is another mask, behind which Shakspere is amusing himself:—

Gru. "Was it fit for a servant to use his master so; being, perhaps, [for aught I see] two-and-thirty,—a pip out?"

Shakspere's manufacturing this comedy out of Marlowe's, and transferring the scene from Greece to Italy, justifies the supposition, that the *Taming of a Shrew* and *Midsummer Night's Dream* were both aimed at the same party. Why Shakspere re-modelled Marlowe's comedy, it is idle guessing, though it may have had some connexion with Lord Southampton, possibly a *feu-de-joie*, that his friend had escaped from the enchantments of this Italian *Circè;* the earl left England in June, having a command in the expedition against Cadiz. "It is," says Mr. Brown, "in the *Taming of the Shrew,* where the evidence is the strongest," that Shakspere had been in Italy.

In Marlowe's comedy, the *Taming of a Shrew,* Fernando is a softened and cocknified Tamburlaine; Aurelius is perhaps intended for Lyly, and Polidor for Shakspere. The comic portion is on a level with the clownage in *Faustus,* and there is only one genuine bit of wit and humour in the whole play, and that comes from the heart and not from the head; at this time, as I have before stated, Marlowe was dependent on the liberality of Southampton and Shakspere; let it be remembered also, that Slie is Christopher Marlowe himself:—

Aurel. "Pardon me, father; humbly on my knees,
I do entreat your grace to hear me speak.
Duke. Peace, villain: lay hands on them,
And send them to prison straight."
[*Phylotus and Valeria* runnes away.
Slie. I say we'll have no sending to prison.
Lord. My lord, this is but the play; they're but in jest.
Slie. I tell thee, *Sim,* we'll have no sending
To prison, that's flat: why, *Sim,* am not I *Don Christo Vary?*
Therefore I say they shall not go to prison.
Lord. No more they shall not, my lord,
They be run away.
Slie. Are they run away, *Sim?* that's well;
Then gis some more drink, and let them play again."

This is the most genuine bit of comedy Marlowe ever wrote, and Shakspere never wrote anything more true to nature; and probably he had this passage in his recollection when he wrote:—

> *Pist.* "Fortune is Bardolph's foe, and frowns on him;
> For he hath stoll'n a *pix*, and hanged must 'a be.
> Damn'd death!
> Let gallows gape for dog, let man go free,
> And let not hemp his windpipe suffocate:
> But Exeter hath given the doom of death,
> For *pix* of little price."—
>
> *Henry V.*, act iii., scene 6.

The *Taming of the Shew* was immediately followed by *King John*, composed most probably during the summer of 1596; whether it was finished, or not, before the death of Hamnet in August, matters little; in Constance we have a picture of the maternal sufferings of Shakspere's wife, anxiously watching the wasting figure of her only son; it may be reasonably inferred such is the case, since no editor pretends, the play was produced before 1595, and in no other play has he painted maternal suffering so vividly and forcibly; and yet the anxiety and misery of Constance are in a measure imaginary; she sees in her mind's eye her son wasting away:—

> *Const.* "There was not such a gracious creature born.
> But now will canker sorrow eat my bud,
> And chase the native beauty from his cheek,
> And he will look as hollow as a ghost;
> As dim and meagre as an ague's fit;
> And so he'll die."—
>
> *King John*, act iii., scene 4.

It may then be inferred, the play was composed in 1596, and brought out probably before the death of Hamnet, if, as Gifford supposes, Jonson has in *Every Man in his Humour* imitated the temptation scene between the King and Hubert.

Towards the end of the year it may be presumed, Shakspere commenced the second part of his great historical drama with *Richard II.*, closely followed by *Henry IV.* and *V.* These latter plays furnish additional evidence that Pistol, like Marlowe, was in his way a learned man. From the incompatibility of the *Merry Wives of Windsor* with these plays, we may be certain it could not have been written at this period; the circumstance of its having been originally composed in 1592, confirms the opinion, Shakspere had in 1590 already sketched in his mind the whole historical drama from *Richard II.* to *Richard III.*

Henry V., it is supposed, was written in 1599; and we may presume Lyly was still living, as Captain Fluellen is twin-brother to Sir Hugh Evans; and his treatment of Pistol reminds us of Lord Lafeu. The polished language of the military pedant, Fluellen, apart from his Welsh Euphuisms, has a remarkable resemblance to the "finished representation of colloquial excellence" of the pedant, Sir Nathaniel, in *Love's Labour's Lost.* These four characters (the two parsons, the lord, and the captain), are composed of the same elements, four brothers at a birth; but they are four individuals quite distinct the one from the other; they are not brothers Cheeryble or Siamese twins, simply because they have not grown up together in the same shop, in the same counting-house; their respected parent, Mr. William Shakspere, was perfectly aware of the influence of education and habit; consequently, the captain and the lord have none of the weakness and nervousness of the two parsons, of Sir Hugh waiting in the field for his enemy, "how full of cholers I am, and trempling of mind," and of Sir Nathaniel, as Alisander, "he is a marvellous good neighbour, insooth; and a very good bowler; but, for Alisander, alas, you see how 'tis;—a little o'erparted."

Soon after this period Nash died, and, it is supposed, Lyly also. Shakspere was now a gentleman in easy circumstances; the owner of New Place, the best house in Stratford, sometimes farming, sometimes playmaking. Some writers, with Hallam at their head, imagine, that in the beginning of the seventeenth century Shakspere must have suffered from :—

> "The proud man's contumely,
> The insolence of office, and the spurns
> That patient merit of the unworthy takes;"

in consequence of *Timon*, the amended *Hamlet*, and *Lear*, having been produced at that period; but others rather lean to the opinion, these characters are purely poetical conceptions, the results of a more extended observation of human life, and unconnected with his personal history; and that he "was never so happy in his own mind as when, by contrast, he was sketching that class of moody characters—Lear, Timon, Jaques, Hamlet, &c., referred to by Mr. Hallam." Jonson's works have been ransacked by Steevens, Malone, and others, in search of spiteful remarks against the mighty dramatist; but it is now generally acknowledged, their accusations and charges against "malignant Ben" have been most ably and satisfactorily refuted by Gifford's caustic pen; and who has not heard of their wit-combats at the *Mermaid*, and of Jonson's eulogy:—

"He was not of an age, but for all time."

Exegi monumentum: I have built me a house, I have written a book; and be it a dream, at least it is not a baseless fabric; it stands on a rock, and not on sand; the genuineness of the documents cannot be doubted, although they may be questioned. I have no theory to defend; "''tis a thing slipped idly from me, as a gum which oozes from whence 'tis nourished;" and though the chaste severity of Shaksperian criticism may be inclined to condemn the whole as a gallimawfry of dreamy supposes, of idle imaginings, yet there are some points that deserve a candid consideration, and challenge the strictest inquiry:—

"And for their sake
Let the rest, if not acceptance take,
At least forgiveness find."

F. PICKTON, PRINTER, PERRY'S PLACE, 29, OXFORD STREET.

www.ingramcontent.com/pod-product-compliance
Lightning Source LLC
Chambersburg PA
CBHW032138160426
43197CB00008B/688